The Open University

A Second Level Course

STUDY GUIDE 1B

ISSUES IN WOMEN'S STUDIES

Prepared for the Course Team by
Diana Gittins, Helen Crowley
and Susan Himmelweit

THE OPEN UNIVERSITY U207 *ISSUES IN WOMEN'S STUDIES* COURSE PRODUCTION TEAM

Amanda Willett, Barbara Hodgson, Catherine King (Chair), Diana Gittins, Dinah Birch, Felicity Edholm, Fiona Harris, Frances Bonner, Gill Kirkup, Harry Dodd, Helen Crowley, Joan Mason, Judy Lown, Kathryn Woodward, Laurie Smith Keller, Linda Janes, Linda McDowell, Lizbeth Goodman, Maggie Riley, Maureen Adams, Meg Sheffield, Melanie Bayley, Randhir Auluck, Richard Allen, Rosemary Pringle, Siân Lewis, Susan Crosbie, Susan Himmelweit, Susan Khin Zaw, Tony Coulson, Veronica Beechey, Wendy Webster

External Assessor: Elizabeth Wilson, Professor of Policy Studies, Polytechnic of North London

The Open University
Walton Hall
Milton Keynes MK7 6AB

First published 1992

Copyright © 1992 The Open University

All rights reserved. No part of this publication may be reproduced, stored in a retrieval system, or transmitted, in any form or by any means, without written permission from the publisher or a licence from the Copyright Licensing Agency Limited. Details of such licences (for reprographic reproduction) may be obtained from the Copyright Licensing Agency Ltd of 33–34 Alfred Place, London WC1E 7DP.

Designed by the Graphic Design Group of The Open University

Printed in the United Kingdom by the Open University

ISBN 0 7492 0105 3

This publication forms part of the Open University course U207 *Issues in Women's Studies*. If you have not enrolled on the course and would like to buy this and other Open University material, please write to Open University Educational Enterprises Ltd, 12 Cofferidge Close, Stony Stratford, Milton Keynes MK11 1BY, United Kingdom. If you wish to enquire about enrolling as an Open University student, please write to the Central Enquiry Office, The Open University, P.O. Box 200, Walton Hall, Milton Keynes MK7 2YZ, United Kingdom.

1.1

Cover illustration by Christine Tacq

3972C/u207sg1bi1.1

CONTENTS

	Preamble	5
	Structure of this Study Guide	5
	Timetabling	6
	Aims	7
	Introduction	8
1	**Chapter 5 Language and difference (Week ~~21~~ 13)**	10
	Introduction	10
	Timetabling	10
	Objectives	10
	Language and feminism	11
	Article 5.1 'Lacan' by Rosalind Minsky	13
	Article 5.2 'Sitting up and lying down: experiences of psychotherapy and psychoanalysis' by Sarah Maguire	20
	Article 5.3 'Images of "woman": the photography of Cindy Sherman' by Judith Williamson	23
	Summary	24
2	**Chapter 6 Subjectivity and identity (Week 22) /4**	25
	Introduction	25
	Timetabling	25
	Objectives	25
	Subjectivity	25
	Article 6.1 'Gender difference and the production of subjectivity' by Wendy Hollway	27
	Article 6.2 'Feminism, criticism and Foucault' by Biddy Martin	31
	Summary	35
3	**Chapter 7 Experience and the politics of identity (Week ~~23~~ 15)**	37
	Introduction	37
	Timetabling	37
	Objectives	39
	Identity	39
	Article 7.1 'Feminism and the challenge of racism ...' by Razia Aziz	41
	Article 7.1 'Multiple mediations ...' by Lata Mani	44
	Article 7.3 'Identity: skin blood heart' by Minnie Bruce Pratt	46
	Summary	46

project work (study wk 15)

4	**Chapter 8 The aims and achievement of feminist theory (Week 31)**	**48**
	Timetabling	48
	Introduction	48
	Artcle 8.1 'The instability of the analytical categories of feminist theory' by Sandra Harding	50
	Article 8.2 'What is feminist theory?' by Elizabeth Gross	54
	References	**55**
	Acknowledgements	**55**

PREAMBLE

At this point, now you have completed Books Two and Three, the work you did for the first part of Book One at the beginning of the course may seem rather distant. If you cast your mind back, you may find it hard to remember much of what it was all about – really, it would be rather surprising if you didn't, considering all the material you've covered since then! Themes you considered in the first part of Book One, however, should now be quite familiar, for they have run through much of the work you did in Books Two and Three: difference; discrimination; sexuality; gender; biology and bodies. You might find it useful nonetheless to refer back briefly to some of your notes and course material for the first four chapters of *Knowing Women*.

STRUCTURE OF THIS STUDY GUIDE

Study Guide 1B covers the last four chapters in Book One, *Knowing Women*. Chapters 5–7 are studied between Book Three and Book Four, and each is one week's work, but Chapter 8 – also covered by this Study Guide – is studied after Book Four, and represents half your week's work in Week 31 before you move on to the Course Conclusion.

This Study Guide has four main sections, each guiding you through a chapter, and each section has guidance on the proportion of time within your week's work to be spent on the elements of that chapter. Most of the sections also have objectives set out to guide you in your study. These can also be used to aid your revision.

There are other elements – such as questions on each part of your reading, key concepts and activities – which you will be familiar with from the previous Study Guides.

TIMETABLING

There are one TV and two radio programmes which will be transmitted during the period of this Study Guide. Make sure that you refer to the Media Notes before you watch/listen to these programmes.

Your timetable for the period covered by this Guide should look like this:

Study Week	*Knowing Women*	Other work
13 ~~21~~	Chapter 5: Language and difference	(TMA 05) TV 4 The Body Social TV 06 Designing production Radio 08 Writing from the — Radio 5 No Sacred Bond. margins
22	Chapter 6: Subjectivity and identity	
14 ~~23~~	Chapter 7: Experience and the politics of identity	
31 (first half)	Chapter 8: The aims and achievement of feminist theory (Course Conclusion)	Radio 11 Women comics: satire and self-image

Summer School also falls at this time, so you may be away during one of the weeks when you are due to be studying these chapters.

AIMS

In the second part of *Knowing Women* we leave more concrete issues for a while and return to consider – and re-consider – some central theoretical questions in greater depth. The purpose of this is both to consolidate our existing work and to pave the way for Book Four, *Imagining Women*. Here the main themes for investigation focus on women as both objects of knowledge and subjects of knowledge. Difference, subjectivity and the politics of identity are the core issues, with a final discussion of what is meant by feminist theory, and where it is going. Specifically, the aims are:

1. To extend and develop the earlier work of Book One on theoretical debates and concepts which are central to contemporary feminism.

2. To develop further earlier work on psychoanalytic theory and in particular the importance of language and symbolization in relation to the construction of women's subjectivity.

3. To examine in more depth the notions of power and of discourse in a consideration of their importance in the construction of subjectivity and identity.

4. To study the relevance and centrality of the politics of difference and identity in feminism.

5. To reflect generally on the creation of knowledge, how this relates to power relations, and what is meant by feminist theory.

INTRODUCTION

In the next two weeks you will be spending a fair amount of time studying some of the ideas of two male theorists: Jacques Lacan and Michel Foucault. Neither of them has made any claim to embracing feminism. Why, you may well ask, are they given space in a course on women's studies?

As you are undoubtedly aware by now, there is no one feminism, but rather several important streams of feminism which, while they converge at times, flow separately in many ways. Socialist feminists, for example, focus attention primarily on women's material conditions, how these conditions exploit and oppress women and how these conditions could be changed. Radical feminists also focus on these issues, but explain them in terms of patriarchy and patriarchal oppression of women by men rather than in terms of economic relations.

Parallel with these, other feminists have sought to understand women's subjectivity and oppression more in terms of psychology. Why, they have asked, if women are oppressed and exploited, don't they resist and rebel more consistently, more powerfully? If heterosexuality is imposed on women, as many argue, why then do so many women still apparently seek heterosexual relationships? If women are exploited by the double shift of childcare and waged work, why do most women still have children? In other words, some feminists have sought answers to how we become who we are not in terms of material conditions, but more in terms of early upbringing, unconscious desires and how these psychological factors affect our subjectivity.

Juliet Mitchell (1974) was the first feminist to 'reclaim' some of Freud's theories after they had been jettisoned during the early days of second wave feminism in revolt against Freud's notion of 'penis envy'. Mitchell believed that psychoanalysis had much to offer feminists, and she was influenced by the ideas of Lacan. Lacan had made important revisions to Freud's theories, notably by arguing that subjectivity, and gendered subjectivity in particular, is acquired as a result of the process by which young children acquire language. Becoming a girl or a boy, therefore, was seen as a symbolic process, and not a biological fact. As such, it was liable to change and it is this facet of Lacan's ideas that has attracted many feminists.

The French feminists Hélène Cixous and Luce Irigaray developed and reinterpreted the theories of Lacan to try and explain the construction of women's subjectivity in a less negative way than Lacan who, they argue, still sees women as 'other'. They focus on the very early months of infancy, the 'pre-Oedipal' period when babies and mothers are closely bonded. This is a time and a relationship which, they argue, has been largely neglected by psychoanalysis. They see it as fundamental to the development of women's subjectivity, mother–daughter relationships and women's sexuality. Nancy Chodorow, whose work you will remember from the first part of Book One, has also argued for more attention to this early period, although she approaches the issue in a different way, putting much more stress on the *social* relationship between children and mothers.

Psychoanalytic feminism, however, has often been criticized by socialist and radical feminists for not placing enough emphasis on the material conditions in which women live out their lives. Whatever unconscious desires may be lurking in us, we still have very different life chances according to our colour, our class, where we were born and where we live. Recently, therefore, more feminists have been drawn to the ideas of Michel Foucault *in conjunction with* psychoanalytical theory to develop a model of ways in which women's subjectivity can be understood as an interactive process between our internal world and the material world in which we live. Foucault's work, as you will remember from Book Two, has been regarded as important by feminists because he sees sexuality as a politically created process, not a fixed entity, and because he sees concepts such as 'woman' as a discourse, not an essential or natural fact or category. This points again to the central importance of language, symbolization and meaning and highlights the possibility of change.

1
CHAPTER 5
LANGUAGE AND DIFFERENCE
(WEEK 21)

INTRODUCTION

Your work this week involves reading Chapter 5 in *Knowing Women*. Here we will consider some key aspects of Lacan's work that have been important for feminists. Of most importance for feminism has been the influence of some of Lacan's ideas on the issue of subjectivity. Lacan's work is extremely complex and abstract and remains controversial. His ideas have also been central to post-modernist theory.

There are a variety of aspects of post-modernist theory. Two in particular have been important for feminists. First, post-modernists have argued that there is no universal 'truth', only a number of discourses purporting to be true, and that therefore there can be no universal theories (referred to as totalizing theories). Meanings and discourses are always in the process of change; what seems true to some individual or group or culture now, may not be true to another individual, group or culture at another time or in another place.

Second, and following from this, because meanings are always mutable, there can never be fixed, universal categories such as 'woman' or 'man'. This contrasts directly with the long-held beliefs of liberal humanism that 'Man' (supposedly encompassing women as well, but modelled by, and on ideals of, men) has certain universal qualities and can develop into a rational, unified and fixed self.

The notion of the unconscious has been central to challenging this. The unconscious by definition is a cluster of irrational forces and, if we accept the arguments of psychoanalytic theory, it is of prime importance in determining our sense of self and our behaviour. In other words, we are who we are, and do what we do, as much as a result of irrational, unconscious forces as by apparently rational ones. We are, in other words, fragmented and contradictory beings, not rational and unified at all.

Article 5.2 by Sarah Maguire is a personal account of her own experiences of psychotherapy and psychoanalysis. It raises interesting issues about the differences between the two approaches and their relative usefulness in helping us to understand ourselves and wider issues of women's subjectivity generally. Williamson's article on the photographic work of Cindy Sherman gives you the opportunity to reflect on questions of subjectivity through representation, a question which is central to the work you will do in Book Four.

TIMETABLING

Your work this week involves reading the introduction to Chapter 5 in *Knowing Women* and the three articles in that chapter. The first article, by Minsky on Lacan, involves some very difficult concepts and I advise you to read it extremely carefully. You should read it more than once. Make sure you have understood it before going on. I suggest, therefore, that you spend at least half your week's study time on this article. The other two essays are much easier reading and can be studied with relative ease and speed.

OBJECTIVES

At the end of the week you should be able to:

1   Understand the relevance of post-modernist theory to women's studies.

2   Give a definition of the unconscious, give examples of its manifestations, and understand its relation in Lacanian theory to language, consciousness and sexual difference.

3   Differentiate between Freud's biologistic model of gendered subjectivity and Lacan's linguistic/symbolic model.

4   Understand language as symbolic with particular reference to signification.

5   Understand how psychoanalytic theory accounts for desire in women and men.

6   Give a basic account of Lacan's theory and contrast it with (a) Freud, and (b) object relations.

7   Explain what is involved in psychotherapy and psychoanalysis and appraise their usefulness.

8   Understand how an 'essential femininity' that is infinitely variable is constructed through different images/representations of women, and how this relates to Lacanian, and post-modern, arguments that there is no unified, rational 'self' or identity.

LANGUAGE AND FEMINISM

The introduction to Chapter 5 deals with the importance of language to feminism over the past few decades and summarizes the central arguments and developments in this area.

Key concepts

difference   the unconscious
subjectivity

Read the Introduction to Chapter 5 and then jot down in a few words what you understand as the main perspectives on the importance of language in feminist theory.

The introduction outlines how, from early on in the women's movement, language was singled out as a central issue that could be seen almost in terms of an index of patriarchal attitudes. Dale Spender, for instance, sees the power of language as essential to patriarchy, while Mary Daly argued that women's liberation should be directed at liberating language. Language as a symbol system has been taken up as a key insight by feminists and psychoanalysts, influenced to a great extent by the work of Lacan. The importance of Lacan's work is that by revising Freud's more essentialist theory of subjectivity, he insisted that it was the symbolizing process of entering language that determined the construction of gendered subjectivity, not the biological difference between male and female genitalia. It is language, according to Lacan, that structures the social subject. Because language and meaning are always changing, this means that the construction of women's subjectivity is also an infinitely permeable process, not rooted in fixed ideas of essential difference. The main points of the introduction, as I saw them, were:

1   Feminists, from the start, regarded language as often sexist and representing women in a negative way.

2   Spender argued that naming is a patriarchal activity, a way in which male power is exercised by 'man-made' language to revile and oppress women.

3   Lakoff studied different ways in which women and men use language and speech and found that, though little girls had a superior ability in language, women were less authoritative in their use of language.

4   Lacan argued that the acquisition of language by children is dependent on understanding sexual difference and that gendered subjectivity is thus tied up with the acquisition of language.

Lacan's ideas have been of great importance in recent years, both to feminist theory and to post-modernism. They have been seen as important because they form a bridge between the realm of the psyche and the social world: the bridge between the two is language. Much of this week will be spent in considering Lacan's theories which almost everybody finds difficult to grasp at first. It's well worth persevering.

▶ **ACTIVITY 1** ◀

Think of situations in your own life where you speak differently – for example, with children, at work, in shops and so on. List as many situations as you can think of.

Now consider your list for a few minutes and answer the following questions:
- In which one of these situations is the 'real' you?
- How do you know?

Most of us find it difficult – impossible – to come up with a clear and definitive answer and this problem of subjectivity – who we think we are – is central to theories of language and psychoanalysis.

Go back to the Introduction to Book One at this point and read the section on subjectivity. Then try to write a definition of the unconscious. If you have any problems, re-read the section on it in Chapter 4 of Book One (pp. 147–8).

Freud found that certain painful/traumatic memories from childhood were inaccessible to the conscious mind because they had been repressed into a hidden area of the mind he called the unconscious. Evidence for its existence he found in people's dreams, jokes and slips of the tongue. The unconscious, according to Freud, is a hidden store of repressed desires, painful memories and images from our pasts which continue to affect our behaviour, indeed our physical health, despite our attempts to deny and repress them.

▶ **ACTIVITY 2** ◀

Think for a few minutes about various reasons why the unconscious and psychoanalysis might be useful for feminism.

One of the central questions for feminism in recent years has been that, having charted how women are oppressed in the material world – as you will have seen clearly in Books Two and Three – why is it, notwithstanding this knowledge, that so many women still accept subordination and oppression? Are we forced into submission by material power relations alone? Or is there something from our earliest experiences that conditions us to (more or less) accept oppression? It is to this latter possibility that many feminists have turned in considering psychoanalytic theory, and the unconscious in particular, as a means of explaining these important questions.

The existence of an unconscious helps to explain the persistence of particular social relations by showing how these are deeply structured into individual inner psyches as well as in outer social institutions. Patriarchy doesn't just exist 'out there' in the material world, but also within our minds, our psyches, our unconscious.

In the early years of second wave feminism there was much hostility to Freud and psychoanalysis, based largely on antipathy to his theory of penis envy. Juliet Mitchell (1974) was one of the first to try and recover aspects of Freudian theory which she believed were important in explaining women's psyches. She drew on the more recent work of Jacques Lacan. Lacan was a practising psychoanalyst in Paris, most of whose work was written between the 1930s and the 1970s. Much influenced by Freud, the most important revision to

Freud that Lacan made was his theory that subjectivity is directly connected to language and the ways in which we learn to use language.

ARTICLE 5.1 'LACAN' BY ROSALIND MINSKY

At this point you need to grapple more thoroughly with the ideas of Lacan himself. They are not easy ideas, but Minsky manages to present them clearly in the article here.

> Now read the beginning of Article 5.1, up to '... satisfying and fulfilling.' (p. 188), considering as you do so:
> (a) the main differences between Freud and Lacan;
> (b) what Klein means by the concept of 'splitting'.

                        Key concepts
      splitting   projection
  object relations

Minsky points out that the main difference between Lacan and Freud is that Lacan draws on theories of linguistics. Lacan's theory is important in that it takes gender difference at a symbolic level, whereas Freud stressed the biological difference more.

Melanie Klein was a contemporary of Freud's and founded the object relations school.

> You should at this point to go back to Book One Chapter 4 (p. 153ff) to refresh your memory of Chodorow, a more recent object relations theorist.

Klein focused more on the period of early infancy than Freud. For her, the instincts were directed towards 'objects' rather than the search for pleasure, as Freud believed. By objects she meant people, or aspects of people. She argued that infants do not simply enter the world with instincts of love and hate but also develop internal images of 'objects' to satisfy these instincts. An infant's first 'object' is usually its mother. This early relationship is characterized by the infant's fantasies that arise from its instincts for love and hate.

The baby begins to take into itself its good experience of love at the breast and to project away from itself and on to the breast its bad experiences of hatred. Initially the baby feels merged with the mother and has no sense of self, but as it becomes aware of the mother as separate these feelings are projected on to her. Thus, according to Klein's theory, we all grow up to some extent with woman-hating psyches, and we all go on to project feelings we don't like about ourselves on to others. This process results in us being 'split' between 'good' and 'bad' feelings.

It is primarily the shift in focus by Klein towards early infancy – the pre-Oedipal phase – and on the relationship between mother and infant that feminists have found useful. This is a period Freud largely ignored. It is a period that has interested the French feminists Kristeva and Irigaray, too, as it is prior to the acquisition of language and is a woman-centred period for both girls and boys. Klein has been criticized, however, for her use of the essentialist notion of 'instinctual drives'.

> Now read to the end of the first paragraph on p. 190 ('... will continue to exist.'), paying particular attention to Lacan's arguments about how the infant first comes to have an early sense of self.

Key concepts
mirror phase   the imaginary

Because babies initially cannot recognize absence, they cannot distinguish between themselves and their environment. Their world is a confused jumble of feelings, physical sensations and a chaotic array of other objects. Around the age of six months they begin to be able to recognize absence and it is at this crucial point that what Lacan calls the 'mirror stage' occurs. I must confess that when I first read about this I was very sceptical and kept thinking of babies in different cultures who wouldn't have access to mirrors. Later I realized that the 'mirror' was a metaphor – that is, not to be taken literally – and then it all began to make more sense.

So the baby sees an image – usually the mother – that it believes to be itself, and falls in love with this apparently ordered image that contrasts with its feelings of chaos. It believes this image to be itself, but in reality it is always an 'other'. So, according to Lacan, this is the kernel of subjectivity. What distinguishes it is the belief that the self we *think* is 'I' isn't in fact, but is who we would like to be. With this changed awareness of self comes a growing awareness of *lack,* an awareness that we are in fact separate from our mother – a feeling which is the genesis of desire and which all of us keep trying to fill, but never can.

> Now read up to p. 192, '... bestow meaning and language.', taking note of:
> (a) how Lacan accounts for the formation of the unconscious;
> (b) what he means by the 'law-of-the-father';
> (c) how he differentiates the phallus from the penis;
> (d) how gendered subjectivity is related to language.
>
> Don't worry if you can't make sense of it all at first; virtually everyone finds Lacan's ideas very hard to grasp to start with.

Key concepts
Oedipus complex/drama   significant/signified
the unconscious   place of the father/law of the father
gendered subject   phallus vs penis

Freud, you will remember, used the myth of Oedipus to explain the phase at which children, both girls and boys, have to renounce their earlier love for their mother. Boys see the father as a rival and fantasize that he will castrate them. This fear is based on the boy's speculation that women, who do not have a penis, have already been castrated by the father. Between the ages of two and three they have to come to terms with the incest taboo of culture, realize that they cannot 'marry mummy', repress their desires for mother into the unconscious where these will be later 'tapped' in transferred love for other women. Girls, according to Freud, come to realize that they lack a penis and 'envy' boys/men. They fantasize that it is their mother who has deprived them of this; they then feel hostility to her and 'transfer' their affection to father.

As well as having initial problems with Lacan's 'mirror', I remember finding Freud's account problematic in the light of families where there was no father present – not just among single-parent families in the Western world but also in other cultures where men live separately or children are raised by grandparents. And what about upper- and middle-class families where children are raised by nannies? Lacan's theory made much more sense because he takes the father at a *symbolic* level. The 'law-of-the-father' is more about social norms, laws, language – becoming part of culture – than about real fathers. Whether or nor a real father is present, all children still have to learn they cannot have everything they want – especially not mother – in an outside world where desire and demands are regulated by roles and laws of which 'father' is a symbol.

The awareness that the child cannot marry its mother results in these desires (largely built on the earlier sense of lack from the mirror phase) being repressed. This, for Lacan, is the point at which the unconscious is formed. It is integral to the child's entry into language. The crucial point here is that entry into language and the formation of the unconscious are both premised on the child's learning about *difference*. Language, a symbol system, is based on difference. 'Up' only has meaning if understood as different from 'down'.

> **ACTIVITY 3**
>
> Think of some other examples.

To enter and understand language all children must understand this 'key' of difference which is the essence of symbolism and thus of language. One thing always stands for something else. The letters 'u.p.' are *signifiers* which put together symbolize, or signify, the concept of 'upness', which is the *signified*, but never the real thing.

Lacan argues that there is one crucial signifier which opens the gate to a child understanding all about difference and thus about language: the phallus. Girls and boys between two and three become aware that mother is not quite like father and the symbol of this difference – in a patriarchal world of the law-of-the-father – is the phallus. While the phallus can represent power in many forms, for children at this stage they (mis)understand it as being the penis. The penis for them embodies the phallus and signifies difference. But, Lacan insists, they are mistaken in this assumption.

The important point here is that the child's entry into language is via an acknowledgement of difference generally and difference between men and women in particular. Part of this awareness is realizing that the child is also part of this difference and either a girl or a boy. Thus to enter culture and language means acquiring gendered subjectivity. It is in this way that Lacan connects the psychic world, the inner world of the unconscious and conscious aspects of an individual, with the social world through language.

> Now read up to '… power to dominate women.' (pp. 192–4), paying close attention to how Lacan explains the different ways in which girls and boys become gendered subjects.

LANGUAGE AND DIFFERENCE

Key concepts

lack   jouissance
desire

'women's entry into culture is experienced as lack'

he wishes he were a *woman*
one of those able to
dance and shake
breasts and belly and hips
loose, a
not-himself, nothing but

he wishes they did not have a
hiding from it in his bed stillness
he bruises easily
he wishes he was still a little boy
so that he did not have to face them
telling him he is an oppressor
he needs them to scold him
darling oppressor
if he were a *woman*

he would join the *women's* movement
but at least his *women* friends
are always *women* who struggle
he has nothing to do but
help them out of
silence, he has
nothing else to do
with *women's* oppression
he wishes they had a *penis* too
so they could all just be friends.

Michele Roberts

I thought this encapsulated some of the arguments against Lacan's notion of a 'negative entry into language/culture' well.

▶ **ACTIVITY 4** ◀

Why do you think Roberts chose to write it from a man's perspective?
How might it have been written from a woman's perspective?
Fill in the blanks!

16

Luce Irigaray has argued that Lacan is phallocentric – i.e. that masculinity, symbolized by the phallus, is always taken as the norm in his theory. She challenges the idea that women 'lack' (the penis, the phallus) and argues that instead of just one sexual organ, women in fact have many and that our bodies have the capacity for our own particular, multiple sexuality. In contrast with the solitary penis, women's 'two lips' give us the chance of a dual and autoerotic sensuality – which she, following Lacan, calls 'jouissance'.

'Jouissance' is almost impossible to translate precisely, but refers to a total joy or ecstacy that Irigaray argues exists outside of linguistic norms. She sees it more as a result of women experiencing the all-over delights of their own bodies than as a specific, genital-focused – and phallocentric – orgasmic pleasure. She sees it as a diffuse and continual form of physical pleasure that women can discover and enjoy for themselves. She also believes that this new pleasure for women could be central in re-evaluating the patriarchal cultural system. Linked to this, she believes women can begin to take apart phallocentric language by writing in a more fluid and 'disturbing' way that draws more directly on their own physicality and unconscious. The French feminist writer Hélène Cixous (1984) shares similar views, believing that writing is a powerful way for women to express difference and thereby to create a feminine input to culture based on, as they see it, women's different embodiment and physical pleasure.

Irigaray has often been criticized as a crude essentialist, given the apparent stress she puts on the different experiences of women as a result of their unique embodiment. Some argue that she thereby ignores the importance of the symbolic. Margaret Whitford (1989), however, believes that for Irigaray the symbolic is vital. The problem is, she argues, that culture has failed to symbolize women's relation to their maternal origins and the relation to the mother's body (and thus all relations between women). This is left unmediated by culture and seen as the place of lack.

But Lacan would argue that women's lack is always socially constructed and that, moreover, lack is central to language. The real subjects are always missing – the letters 'c.a.t.' can never be a real cat. Both girls and boys feel lack and this feeling of lack is how *desire* is created. Having lost the mother as love object, both girls and boys keep trying to fill the resultant gap/lack they feel – the real object of which has been repressed into the unconscious. They think the phallus will fill the gap, but this, according to Lacan, is an illusion, for the phallus is only a signifier, a symbol – and a symbol of the loss of the mother and not of the penis.

The real subject of desire for both girls and boys (that is, the mother) is thus always beyond consciousness. As a result we always feel that yearning, that desire, that lack – but we never interpret it consciously as desire for the mother. Instead it focuses on a multiplicity of different objects that we think we desire. But we are rarely really satisfied – because none of them is *really* what we desire in our unconscious.

▶ **ACTIVITY 5** ◀

Try to think of some objects you find desirable. For me these would include chocolate (the darkest, covering truffles, hazelnuts and marzipan in particular), a tropical beach (minus Telly Savalas), a slim body (my own; notice the contradiction with the first objects), tabby kittens.

Think of ways in which advertising plays on these desires to sell consumer goods.

Now read to '... I think where I am not.' (on p. 196), bearing in mind the ways in which psychoanalysis finds evidence for unconscious desires and feelings. Think of some examples from your own experience of situations or 'Freudian slips' where your real wishes that you would rather have concealed were blurted out. The next article, by Sarah Maguire, will give some particularly good examples.

For me, I remember one incident in particular, towards the end of a rather unhappy marriage. We had had a big row and were trying to make it up, trying to make the other feel (or at least I was) that everything really could be OK again. 'Darling' I murmured in his ear, 'I really do loathe you.' As I said, the marriage didn't last much longer.

▶ **ACTIVITY 6** ◀

Think back to the preliminary exercise for the week where you listed situations where you speak differently. Could you now add any other situations?

COMMENT

Perhaps you might add the 'I' of dreams, or the 'I' that meant to say 'love' but said 'loathe' instead – examples of the unconscious at work. Lacan asks the question if there is any way all these different aspects of ourselves might be summed up. His answer is *no*, never. This belief that there is no single, unified self is at the core of post-modern theory. If, as feminists, we accept this premise that there is no single, unified self, we can use this to get away from essentialist notions of 'woman'. By so doing, it becomes possible to acknowledge the diversity of women. But it is also problematic because if carried to its logical conclusion it means there is no such thing as 'woman' and, if this is the case, what is the point of a women's movement? It is a problem you will be aware of already and which will be addressed in Chapters 7 and 8 particularly.

Read to '... to be a hoax.' on p. 199 and then answer the following questions.
What price do girls pay for 'lack'?
What price do boys pay for 'symbolic castration'?

Key concept
binary opposition

Girls, mistaking the penis for the phallus, think they can 'get' the phallus from future (male) lovers. But the phallus is in fact an illusion that veils the unconscious desire that was originally for the mother but is now mistakenly believed to be for the penis via male lovers.

Boys, on the other hand, always have to feel desired by women as a disguise for the original hurt of loss and fear they might be castrated. In other words, men have to have women's sense of lack – which they (mis)interpret as the need for male lovers – for their own desires to be desired by women to be met. So men can only feel powerful if women desire them, that is, desire the phallus they feel they lack.

And what if women cease to desire male lovers as a (mistaken) route to the phallus?

According to Minsky's interpretation, male power and patriarchy collapse.

▶ **ACTIVITY 7** ◀

Try to think of some concrete examples where women have made it apparent that they do not desire men and the phallus. How do men in such situations react?

COMMENT

Examples could include any kind of situation where women choose to exclude men. Greenham Common is a good example. At the beginning, there were often very acrimonious debates about whether to exclude men from the camp. The exclusion of men was much resented by many men and harassment was a not infrequent occurrence. Often I have found in courses I have tutored that putting students in single-sex groups, while generally very freeing for the women, creates a great deal of resentment and protest from the men. I have noticed time and again in such situations, too, that whereas women then talk a great deal more, and more openly, men tend to withdraw, say less, even sulk.

> Read to '... and exceeds it.' on p. 200 and make notes on how women can have an identity within the framework of Lacan's theory.

Key concept
masquerade

Basically, the answer seems to be only with the greatest difficulty, if at all. Women's initial 'entry into language/culture' and their resultant sense of lack is doubled by men projecting *their* own sense of lack on to women through belittlement. It's all part of binary opposition which is so central to language itself and suggests that women are *opposite* to men as up is opposite to down. In fact, it's difficult to see how women could be *opposite* to men – only different. The problem with binary opposition, on which so much of our culture is based, is that one term always tends to be positive, while the other is negative. No prizes for guessing which one in the man/woman dichotomy.

For Lacan, heterosexuality – 'natural feminine behaviour' – is a masquerade consisting of acting out roles set by patriarchy. It is an argument that was made in the 1920s by the psychoanalyst Joan Riviere, who argued in an article called 'Womanliness as masquerade' that women who wish for masculinity often put on a mask of womanliness to avert anxiety and the retribution feared from men. Luce Irigaray, more recently, commented that the masquerade is what women do in order to participate in men's desire, but at the cost of giving up their own.

▶ ACTIVITY 8 ◀

Think of some of the words men use to label women, such as 'bimbo'. List as many as you can think of. Now think of all the words you can to label men. Compare them.

I find it easy to think of words for 'woman' – Madonna, whore, slag, bitch, career woman, bluestocking, dyke – some of which almost all of us will have experienced being called at some time or other. Not generally a very pleasant experience either. But for men – well, macho, male chauvinist pig, medallion man. None of these has the same force and ready images as those for women. Looking at the words for women, note how the only one that is positive, Madonna, represents an impossible ideal: a woman who bore a child without any sexual contact at all. Note how almost all of these words carry sexual innuendo. We shall be considering this in more detail in Williamson's article on Cindy Sherman's photography. It all points to serious problems of identity and autonomy for women because arguably these stereotypes/representations are created by men, by patriarchy, to categorize women. It is hard to define our own selves within these stereotypes. Post-modernist theory makes it even harder by saying we haven't got any selves anyway. Thanks, Jacques.

Now read to the end of the article (pp. 200–05) and make a list of both the positive and negative aspects, as you understand them, of Lacan's theory.

For Lacan:
- The links he makes between the unconscious, language and culture explain a great deal about how the development of gendered subjectivity takes place. In this way he makes an important link between the inner, psychic world and social processes.
- His theory, unlike that of Freud, is not ultimately premised on biological assumptions. By focusing as he does on the importance of language and symbolism, this pitfall is avoided.
- He suggests how notions of femininity and masculinity which are tied up in gendered subjectivity are ephemeral, precarious, based on false assumptions.
- Change for women is a much greater possibility because so much operates at a symbolic level. Language can change, so can meaning.

Against Lacan:
- Women have no identity and only appear in 'masquerade'. Women (and men) are 'de-centred', denied as subjects just at a time when women are trying to claim that they *are* subjects in their own right and not just 'other' to men or defined by men.
- His notion of 'woman' is based on a very narrow idea of difference – that is, just difference between men and women. Differences exist *between* women as well as *within* women.
- The notion of 'lack' could be seen to be a disguise for penis envy. Why should that one solitary organ be so important? Is there still space for womb envy? What about Irigaray's ideas about 'multiple sexuality'?

Whatever you may think of Lacan's arguments – you may agree with some and disagree with others – it is important to realize how they have influenced feminist theory dramatically in the past few years. They challenged pre-existing notions of subjectivity and essentialist ideas of 'woman'. They have also drawn attention to the significance of our irrational selves, the complicated influences on behaviour of the unconscious, and the complex and frequently contradictory processes that define our sexuality.

ARTICLE 5.2 'SITTING UP AND LYING DOWN: EXPERIENCES OF PSYCHOTHERAPY AND PSYCHOANALYSIS' BY SARAH MAGUIRE

Minsky ends her article by suggesting that self-knowledge, acquired presumably through psychotherapy/psychoanalysis, could be an important way for women to challenge and empower themselves. The next article is an account by Sarah Maguire of her own experiences in psychotherapy and psychoanalysis.

► **ACTIVITY 9** ◄

Before you start to read the next article, jot down in a few words:
Your ideas or impressions about what psychotherapy/analysis actually involves.
What are your own feelings about it? If you haven't experienced it already, how would you feel about doing so?
Key ways you can remember in which we can find evidence of the contents of the unconscious

> Key concept
> transference

> Now read Article 5.2, 'Sitting up and lying down ...' by Sarah Maguire.
>
> As you read it, be aware of examples in the text of some of the theoretical points you have just studied in the previous essay. These would include, for instance: evidence of her unconscious wishes and desires; aspects of her gendered subjectivity such as her sexual preferences; early experiences that might have affected her later patterns of behaviour.

Hopefully, you found it enjoyable and had no difficulty in picking out her physical symptom: psoriasis. Freud would have called this an 'hysterical' symptom, a physical manifestation of her unconscious screaming for help – a kind of warning light.

> Can you think of other examples from literature or the media?

I thought of Denis Potter's television serial, *The Singing Detective*, which also featured psoriasis, and Maya Angelou's autobiography, *I Know Why the Caged Bird Sings*, where sexual abuse by an uncle led to her being unable to speak for several years.

► **ACTIVITY 10** ◄

Maguire's therapy was based on the ideas of Winnicott, of the object relations school. Both Klein and Chodorow also subscribe to this school. Bearing in mind Chodorow's main ideas from Chapter 4, write down a few sentences that clarify the difference between the ideas of the object relations school and those of (a) Freud and (b) Lacan.

Object relations theorists put much more emphasis on the early relationship between mother and infant than does Freud. They are interested more in the pre-Oedipal phase than is Freud, who focuses first and foremost on the Oedipal phase. The object relations school focuses more on the quality of relationships between infant and carer rather than on innate drives. Lacan pays *some* attention to the pre-Oedipal world through his theory of the mirror phase. But his main focus, like Freud, is on the Oedipal stage as the time when the child enters language, learns difference and acquires gendered subjectivity. Lacan is different from both the object relations school and Freud in stressing the importance of language and the symbolic.

> What were the main differences between therapy and analysis for Maguire?

Transference is the most crucial aspect of psychoanalysis. It describes the feelings of the analysand (that is, the person being analysed) for her analyst. These feelings are constantly challenged and discussed, for they are the analysand's projections of much earlier feelings for parents. Through these the analysand comes to grasp very early feelings of desire, betrayal, rage, love for her parents. This bringing to consciousness of repressed unconscious feelings from childhood is how the cure is supposed to be brought about.

> In what other ways did the unconscious manifest itself?

Through resisting the analyst's insights; gaps; silences.

ACTIVITY 11

What did you think about Maguire's account of her own racism? Would it be a valid strategy to tackle racism at a personal level rather than a political, institutional one? Jot down a few ideas on this.

COMMENT

Racism exists at several levels. Most obviously it permeates social institutions and the very structure of society itself. This is more obvious, of course, in countries like South Africa, but no doubt you can think of several ways in which racism imbues British institutions. Research has shown, for instance, how people of colour and from minority ethnic groups are time and again disadvantaged in both the labour market and the housing market. Racist stereotypes often occur in the media and, indeed, in language. Some degree of racism can be dealt with through changing social policy and legislation. But racism also exists at an individual level, in both our conscious and unconscious minds. Consciously, most of us deplore and condemn racism and racist politics, as did Sarah Maguire. At an unconscious level, however, we may still unwittingly retain irrational fears of others who seem different to us. These can, and often do, conflict with our conscious beliefs. Working with our own prejudices at a personal level helps to elucidate and dispel these irrational fears and prejudices. Even if everyone, including neo-Nazis and the Ku-Klux Klan, tackled their unconscious racism, however, I think we would still need to deal with the problem in more organized and structural ways to tackle the racism inherent in social institutions themselves. Ideally, therefore, I think we need both.

> How did you feel about Maguire's 'gender' difficulties' that triggered off her depression – and her psoriasis?

The women's movement has often been divided about issues relating to sexuality and sexual orientation in particular. Radical feminists have argued that lesbianism is the only effective way to resist male oppression and patriarchy. Adrienne Rich wrote a famous article called 'Compulsory heterosexuality and the lesbian continuum' in which she argues that heterosexuality is actually enforced on women who, because of their initial relationship with their mother, would, if left alone, prefer women. She argues that this initial relationship means *all* women are on a 'lesbian continuum' of woman-identified experience that may, but need not necessarily, be expressed sexually. Radical feminists like Rich, Charlotte Bunch and Ti-Grace Atkinson argue that lesbian feminism involves both a sexual preference and a political choice, in that it rejects male definitions of women's lives. They attack both the institution and the ideology of heterosexuality, which they see as being at the centre of patriarchy and a patriarchal society.

Maguire's account of her analysis shows an apparently caring analyst who was able to alleviate her suffering and facilitate her self-knowledge. Unfortunately not everyone is so lucky. There are many instances of women (in the United States in particular) who were survivors of sexual abuse and who were then abused by male therapists.

> What other criticisms might be made of therapy and analysis?

They are expensive. Though some can get it on the NHS, not everyone can and, if you do, you often have little choice as to who you work with. They are highly individualistic: much depends on the quality and goodwill of the individual therapist. Not everyone can cope with the pain and difficulties that are usually entailed. Not everyone can spare the time and emotional effort.

Both Maguire and Minsky are very positive about the benefits of therapy and analysis for women – indeed, suggest it could be an important political step for women. Do you think it could be a substitute for, or an addition to, more conventional political action? Could it change the severe oppression of so many women in developing countries?

ACTIVITY 12

Are your feelings about therapy/analysis now, having read the article, any different from the ones you jotted down in answer to Activity 9 before you read it?

ARTICLE 5.3 'IMAGES OF "WOMAN": THE PHOTOGRAPHY OF CINDY SHERMAN' BY JUDITH WILLIAMSON

In Sarah Maguire's essay she recounts how during therapy she altered her style of dress – and then, later, her sexual orientation – in a general move towards change. Elizabeth Wilson once said, 'I don't know who I am until I'm dressed'. Clothes, appearance, image are usually of vital importance to us in defining who we think we are/would like to be/think others want us to be. In the next article Williamson considers some of these issues in relation to the photography of Cindy Sherman.

► ACTIVITY 13 ◄

Before reading the article, take some time to study the photographic images – bearing in mind that Sherman posed for all of them herself. Try to answer the following questions:
As a group, what do you think the photos are about?
How do you feel about them?
Which image, or images, comes closest to your idea of 'femininity'? Why?
Think about ways in which you could use photography for your project on biography or autobiography.

Now read Article 5.3, paying careful attention to the images as you do so. What does Williamson mean by Sherman's 'elision of image and identity'?

I think she means that the only identity is in the way a viewer views the image – i.e. we pour our own meanings, stereotypes on to other women's images. Thus it is the image, the representation, that is 'feminine' – and not the actual woman.

► ACTIVITY 14 ◄

Think of an example from your own experience of when you stereotyped a woman according to (how you interpreted) her image and then realized later she was actually quite different to what you originally thought. Are men less vulnerable to this process? Why?

I think men are much less so – perhaps because they tend to dress much more uniformly. Obviously, there are distinctions – Gothics, Skins, Yuppies etc. – but none of these seems to have the same emotional or sexual connotations as do stereotypes of women. Williamson sees our responses as emotional reactions from within our own selves that we project on to images. This, she argues, is how *ideology* works. The face is the clue, or trigger, to the emotion. That it apparently works much more forcibly for women suggests that is is very much patriarchal ideology that is at work.

How does Williamson see Sherman's images as relating to femininity?

She suggests that we fit the stills into our own narrative and thereby give them meaning. The narratives we have available will presumably also be stereotypes. She also sees the images as linked with vulnerability and eroticism – which are usually the content of available narratives in our culture on women. They are, therefore, something *forced* on women. You might like to consider how this might relate to arguments and issues about pornography – which will be discussed in Book Four.

▶ **ACTIVITY 15** ◀

Jot down a few ideas on how Cindy Sherman's work could be seen as influenced by the theories of Lacan.

Sherman is attacking the notion of an 'essential' self or femininity. While each image could be seen to represent the 'essential feminine', the fact that there are many images shows this idea of the essential femininity to be a lie. This is brought home by the fact that Sherman models for each image. This could be seen to relate to Lacan's argument that there is no essential, unified self. Femininity, he argues, is a 'masquerade'.

SUMMARY

1. We are all divided between the unconscious and consciousness. Evidence for the unconscious comes through dreams, slips of the tongue, silences and, in psychoanalysis, transference. Lacan sees the unconscious as being formed during the process of acquiring language and rationality, a process that is inherent to the acquisition of gendered subjectivity.

2. Language is a symbolic system based on signification crucial to which are difference and lack.

3. The phallus is the central signifier of the entry to language based on difference and as such is symbolic of the law-of-the-father.

4. The phallus is mistakenly thought by boys and girls to be synonymous with the penis. However, the two are not as distinct as Lacan suggests.

5. Girls, according to Lacan, enter language and culture negatively – because they think they 'lack' the phallus. Later, they try to 'get' it by 'masquerading' to men whom they believe have the phallus.

6. Men try to 'prove' they have the phallus, which they actually fear they haven't because of repressed castration phantasies, by needing adoration from women who also (mistakenly) believe that men have the phallus.

7. Desire in both girls and boys is constructed by infantile feelings of loss and lack – rooted in the initial loss of the mother – which is always repressed in the unconscious and (re)interpreted as desire for other, different objects – which never ultimately satisfy the desire.

8. In post-modern theory there is no unified self. Sherman's work in particular shows how the notion of an essential femininity is untenable.

9. Lacan's theory, though very important in stressing the changeability of meaning, still results in a very negative and limited way of seeing women – taken to its logical conclusion, women as such cannot exist, can only be an 'other' for men. This neglects differences between women and within women themselves.

2
CHAPTER 6
SUBJECTIVITY AND IDENTITY
(WEEK 22)

INTRODUCTION

This week the main reading is Chapter 6 of *Knowing Women*. There are two articles, in addition to the introduction. They are concerned with the issues of subjectivity, power and discourse and both will need quite careful reading.

In the first article Wendy Hollway considers how and why we take up certain 'subject positions' in the construction of our subjectivity. Drawing on Lacanian theory, she argues that we need to see the creation of subjectivity not just as a result of unconscious desires, but as an interplay between these and discourses that permeate the historical, social and political contexts of our lives.

In Biddy Martin's article you will encounter concepts influenced by the work of Foucault, whom you have already come across in Chapters 2 and 3 of Book One. Foucault was a prolific writer and here you will have the chance to consider in more depth some of his ideas on discourse, as well as on power. He has been important for feminist theory not only for his work on power and the history of sexuality, but because his idea that 'woman' is a discourse created by others has had important ramifications for the whole issue of subjectivity and identity.

TIMETABLING

The work for this week is drawn from Chapter 6 of Book One. It consists of two articles and quite a long introduction to the chapter. I suggest that you read the introduction right through once, then read the articles themselves. After that it would be a good idea to re-read the introduction. Time for the two articles should be divided roughly equally.

OBJECTIVES

By the end of the week you should be able to:

1. Define 'discourse' and give a variety of examples.
2. Drawing on Foucauldian theory, understand both how unconscious desire can be socially mediated and that power is central to the construction of subjectivity.
3. Be able to account for how we come to occupy certain subject positions within discourses.
4. Understand the connections between power and sexuality in Foucauldian theory.
5. Be able to account for the process of 'splitting' through projection and introjection in heterosexual relations.
6. Understand the dilemma that post-structuralist deconstruction of the term 'woman' implies for feminism.

SUBJECTIVITY

By now, you are probably very familiar with the issue of subjectivity, and how we become who we (think we) are. Sociologists, particularly in the early days of second wave feminism, argued that we become who we are entirely through socialization – our parental upbringing, our education, our exposure to the media and so on. Subjectivity, in other words, was seen as a result of social construction alone. Psychoanalytical theory, and Lacanian theory in particular, drew more attention to the realm of the unconscious and how entry to language and the symbolic was crucial in the construction of a gendered subjectivity. Psychoanalytic theory, however, pays little attention to the historical, social and political contexts in which we negotiate our lives and selves. It is to this problem that the following articles are largely addressed, and which Crowley summarizes in the introduction to Chapter 6. As suggested above, you might well want to re-read the introduction after you have read the rest of the chapter.

> Read the Introduction (pp. 235–9), bearing in mind the following questions:
>
> What can impede our conscious aims and desires?
>
> Does Lacan's theory foreclose feminism?
>
> How does Foucault see power in relation to subjectivity?

Key concepts

discourse   hegemonic discourse

As you will remember from reading Article 5.2, Maguire's conscious political principles of sexual choice and anti-racism were apparently subverted by her unconscious fears and desires. She had to negotiate a way between these two contradictory forces. It could be argued, then, that her subjectivity was formed by social, economic and political forces within a particular historical context *as well as* by her unconscious wishes and desires.

You might like to refresh your memory of the critiques of Lacan from last week. Basically, his definition of 'woman' as negative can be taken to mean that there is no such thing as 'woman' and this denies the possibility of a sense of self, identity, political action based on the notion of 'women' or 'women's needs/oppression'. Lacan's theory has also been criticized as ahistorical and, in certain ways, essentialist. The reason for this criticism is that he implies that the unconscious and its processes are universal. Although we can never know for sure, it seems likely that the content and even the process of the unconscious and its formation may vary over time and between cultures where childrearing practices and culture itself are very different from our own.

Much of the work this week is focused around the ideas of Michel Foucault and how they might be usefully combined with the theory of Lacan in feminist thought.

▶ **ACTIVITY 16** ◀

You should remember Foucault from Book Two and it would be a good idea now to go back and refresh your memory.

Power, for Foucault, is central to the construction of subjectivity. He never sees power as something one person, class or gender 'has' and the other(s) hasn't. Power he sees as being constantly constituted and reconstituted through social interactions and relationships. There is a power relationship when a baby refuses to eat or throws its toys on the floor, just as there is when the government passes laws on abortion or taxation. The principal way in which power operates is through 'discourses'. Some discourses at any time will be particularly dominant; these are what are often called 'hegemonic discourses'. The concept of 'hegemony' was used by the Italian sociologist Gramsci with reference to the ways in which ideological processes permeated social institutions to support the ruling groups of society. Here it is used in terms of how one discourse can become more dominant, that is more important, than others. In other words, it is used to describe how a body (or certain bodies) of beliefs, concepts and representations are promulgated as 'normal', 'true' and 'natural' from a number of social institutions. An example of this would be how scientific discourse, following Darwin, challenged existing discourse (largely religious) about the origins of humanity.

> ## ACTIVITY 17
> Jot down a few notes on what you think might be examples of hegemonic discourses in our society.

COMMENT

One might well be the discourse that defines heterosexual sex as 'natural' and marriage as 'normal' – a patriarchal discourse. Medical discourse could be another. Medical discourse, for instance, defines all physical symptoms as needing scientific/medical definition and attention, rather than emotional/psychotherapeutic or spiritual help. Maguire's psoriasis is a good example here: it was originally treated medically and only through her mother's intervention was presented as possibly being a symptom of an emotional problem.

A discourse is a body of beliefs, terms, specialist language that purports to be 'true' within its own sphere. It is something imposed on everyone, largely through language via 'factual' statements, rules and norms. The discourse of heterosexual marriage, for instance, is presented (in many different forms and institutions) as natural, normal and desirable, for exampe 'love and marriage go together like a horse and carriage'. Many accept and believe these tenets (or some of them) as 'true'. Feminist discourse, however, does not see them as true. Feminist discourse has its own truths on these questions which contradict and challenge the other. For Foucault, meaning is never fixed, but always changing and always open to challenge.

Subject positions are created by discourses. So Cindy Sherman's images could be seen as representations of different subject positions within patriarchal discourse on women. The problem Hollway examines is how we come to occupy some subject positions and not others. Subject positions are many and varied and we may hold several simultaneously, often scarcely being aware of our position(s). The ways in which we come to hold these positions are complex and often contradictory, but, Hollway would argue, in the end determine why some of us have children while others do not, why some of us have certain jobs or prioritize some aspects of our lives over others, and so on.

ARTICLE 6.1 'GENDER DIFFERENCE AND THE PRODUCTION OF SUBJECTIVITY' BY WENDY HOLLWAY

Now read Article 6.1, pp. 240–42 to '... I preserved my difference.', taking note of how she managed to preserve her difference.

Key concept
difference

Hollway criticizes early theories that made women define women negatively in an effort to be 'as good as men'. This encapsulates the whole problem of otherness – first raised by de Beauvoir (see Chapter 1) – which we have been considering in relation to Lacan's theory. Being a 'person' in a male-dominated environment such as work often means operating within that particular, male-dominated, discourse of values and 'truth'. These will generally be negative about women. To resolve this problem, Hollway played out a conventional 'feminine' role in the context of a heterosexual relationship.

ACTIVITY 18

Reflect for a moment on your own life and ways in which you may have experienced conflicts between different discourses on appropriate behaviour or 'truths'.

COMMENT

One obvious conflict for me has been between my 'mothering self' and my 'academic self' where, to do a job well, I need to appear rational, in control and often should give extra time to my work. The demands of my daughter, the notion that I should always be 'there' for her and make her needs top of my list sometimes clash dramatically with my extra-familial work – for example when the school play was on at the same time as an important meeting.

I think the following poem brings some of this question to light.

Place tabs in Slots

What you see here, ladies and gentlemen,
is not me
It is a life-size, cardboard stand-up cut-out
bearing my features,
my interested smile and shiny shoes.
It talks too:
when you say this
it says that
and when you say that
it says this –
or something that, to be
extra agreeable in good company.
But I am elsewhere, off
on my own tack.
I do many things behind your backs –
even die dramatically on occasions –
and no-one notices. My smile
never slips out of place.
I'm good at this
(and that)
so long as I don't actually have to be there.
I wonder why you haven't noticed?
Come to think of it
you never do.
In fact there's something curiously
one-dimensional about you which
begins to disturb me ...

Sylvia Kantaris

Smiling, it seems to me, is a central tenet of patriarchal discourse on femininity. I like the poem because it seems to me to capture that feeling of having to 'step into' a certain self or disguise for specific occasions that never feels like the 'real me'. The problem remains of whether there is such a thing as a real me in the first place. I find it comforting to think there is, but post-modernist discourse would have no hesitation in telling me I'm sadly mistaken.

> Now read the section entitled 'Gender differences in three discourses concerning sexuality' (pp. 242–50), taking note of the concept of discourse and, in particular, whether you agree with the discourses Hollway singles out for discussion.

Key concepts

subject position   totalizing theory

One of the most innovative aspects of Foucault's theory is that it allows scope for contradictory discourses to co-exist at any point in time. This represents quite a change from earlier 'totalizing' theories of, for instance, Marx or Freud which tended to explain a given phenomenon or historical period in terms of *one* principal factor that (more or less) determined everything else. In this way Foucault would certainly take issue with patriarchy which, to a greater or lesser degree depending on the particular theorist, sees men/masculinity/male power as the ultimate cause of women's oppression.

In an interview, Foucault once compared the ideas in his latest book to a piece of Gruyère cheese: there were holes in it which the readers could fill in for themselves. He was opposed to all 'totalizing' theories because for him there was never any ultimate truth about anything; 'truth' was constantly being created and re-created within discourses.

> Think about how a discourse differs from a theory. (You might like to go back to the section on theory in the Course Introduction (Section 5).)

As I see it, a theory is more specifically concerned with explanation than a discourse. A theory sets out to try and explain, or account for, a certain phenomenon, such as poverty, while a discourse is a more general and even random collection of beliefs, theories and 'truths' within a broader sphere of knowledge or practice. So we can talk about a medical discourse which includes a huge number of theories and beliefs and practices, but the idea of a 'theory of medicine' is too all-encompassing; instead we would talk about theories of childbirth or kidney malfunction and so on.

▶ ACTIVITY 19 ◀

Hollway claims that discourses 'make available positions for subjects to take up'. Think of different positions within, say, her 'have/hold' discourse. Jot them down. Then make a few notes on why you think different positions are taken up by different women.

COMMENT

Subject positions within the have/hold discourse might include: a married career woman/superwoman; a full-time housewife and/or mother; a victim of marital cruelty/violence. Reasons might include: past experience and unconscious desires; class background; educational background; personal ambition; ethnic background; age. Foucault himself says very little about these kinds of factors. It's a valid criticism to be levelled at him.

> Think back for a moment to Maguire's essay and reflect on the extent to which Hollway's approach might help to explain it. What were the main discourses for Maguire? And how did these affect her desire?

For me the two discourses on sexuality, which competed with and contradicted one another, were the most obvious. Her desire seemed to be for a heterosexual orientation, while her conscious mind, influenced by feminist discourse, rejected this. It might, however, also be relevant to consider the relative power and influence of the two discourses. It could be argued that the strength of patriarchal discourse on heterosexuality is so powerful throughout our culture – very much a hegemonic discourse – that constantly to resist it is exhausting, difficult and painful. What do you think?

► **ACTIVITY 20** ◄

Hollway agrees that Lacan's idea of 'desire for the other' (which, you will remember, was ultimately, unconsciously, desire for the mother) reasserts itself in adult heterosexual relationships. Pick out a few key quotes from the article which you feel substantiate this.

COMMENT

All of them could be said to show this to some extent, but Jim's was probably the most obvious, viz: 'There's a gaze of uncritical, totally accepting love... and that's a mother's gaze.' The proof of this was in peeling the orange.

► **ACTIVITY 21** ◄

Now write down a few lines about the process of how women and men position themselves in heterosexual relationships.

COMMENT

Dominant discourses define men as needing to be powerful, rational and so on while women are defined as everything men are *not* supposed to be (weak, emotional, vulnerable etc.). So for a couple to seem 'normal' according to this discourse, they (try to) take up gender differentiated positions according to these qualities. By doing so, however, they suppress their own needs and desires which are defined as 'other' by the discourse. So Hollway sees the reproduction of gender differentiated positions and practice as depending on the discourses within which heterosexual relationships are made.

Now read through to the end of Article 6.1 (pp. 250–74), taking note of what you understand Hollway means by the concept of splitting.

Key concepts

splitting   introjection
projection

As I see it, it is the process described briefly above where, by taking up certain positions in the dominant discourse on gender differentiation within heterosexual relationships, women put on to their partner – project – all those attributes of themselves which they deem inappropriate to the discourse on femininity. And vice versa for men. These positions are then defined as 'natural' or part of their different 'personalities'.

Try to describe how power relationships operate in this process of splitting.

They seem to operate largely through binary opposition, so if one shows feelings, then the other must be the 'opposite' and be a strong supporter. But these very oppositions are part of a historical discourse that has defined them as opposites. If you think about it, there's not really that much that is opposite between feeling and support, not in the way east is opposite to west.

SUBJECTIVITY AND IDENTITY

> ## ACTIVITY 22
> Many of the opposites we take for granted really aren't opposite at all. Try to think of some examples.

COMMENT

Women and men, obviously. Active and passive. Feeling and thought. Sensitive and rational. The 'oppositeness' of these has been socially constructed historically – all that can really be said is there are differences between them. Placed as they tend to be in opposition to one another, however, one is always weighted with more positive value.

Splitting is a good example of how something that is actually socially constructed comes to be defined as, and to feel, 'natural'. Will and Beverley's discussion about abortion is a good example. I think the crucial part of Hollway's point here is how she argues that Lacanian theory ignores the content of what is repressed in the unconscious, while discourse analysis provides a way of understanding the content of the splitting in a historical and social context. So our position within discourse is largely determined by the interface between our unconscious desires and an aspect of a discourse which seems, at an unconscious level, to satisfy these desires (but never really can). This operates largely through the processes of projection and introjection.

> How do you understand the terms 'projection' and 'introjection'?

Basically, they're about how repressed desires are put onto, and then taken in by, others. So Will projected on to Beverley what he saw as his weak and vulnerable aspects – those parts of himself that contradicted what he saw as his position within the wider discourse of masculinity. She introjected these, took them into her own definition of her position within the discourse and in turn projected her own unacceptable characteristics on to Will. So they complemented each other, in a way, but only by denying important aspects of themselves.

> Does this process ring true for you? What problems might there be with this theory?

It is only, of course, about heterosexual relationships. I wonder how the process would operate in a lesbian relationship, especially if partners don't position themselves as 'butch/femme'. What about a relationship where one partner is bisexual, or where both are? Hollway doesn't claim that her theory has any application other than to heterosexual relationships, though she could be criticized for only considering these and thereby implying that these are 'normal' relationships.

Perhaps the most important argument of Hollway is that contradictions in subject positions and relationships can be challenged and changed – as we saw in Maguire's essay. Psychoanalytic theory, then, according to Hollway, because it fails to account for the historical context within which we live out our lives and the various discourses that confront us in that process, does not account adequately for subjectivity. Only by using it in conjunction with the Foucauldian concept of discourse does she believe it can work.

ARTICLE 6.2 'FEMINISM, CRITICISM AND FOUCAULT' BY BIDDY MARTIN

> Now read pp. 275–6 of Article 6.2 up to '... the implications of his work.', and jot down what you understand to be Foucault's concept of power.

Power, according to Foucault, is everywhere. It is constituted in all social situations and in our very bodies. It is not something one person has and another lacks, nor something the state has and all the rest of us lack. There is no 'essence' to power; there are as many forms of power as there are relationships between people, discourses and institutions. Everybody is subject to power, and everybody has the ability to exercise it. Even a baby, in all its helplessness and dependence on adults, still is able to resist to some extent, to exert its own power, by screaming, crying, writhing or wriggling in protest.

Moreover, power isn't just repression, it isn't just about making someone do something they don't want to, it's also 'enabling'. By that Foucault means it is also positive; we use the power from knowledge to change things, for instance. Power and knowledge are intimately connected. Knowledge is actually a *part* of power and power relations, and thus all knowledge is also political. If you know, for instance, that x stole y, that knowledge gives you the power to apprehend/challenge them or to enable them to escape. Power, according to Foucault, is something produced by the relation between pleasures (or desires) and knowledge and is constantly being produced and re-produced in a myriad of ways.

> Now read up to p. 279 ('... to plague leftist thinking and strategy.') and make notes as you read on the connections Foucault makes between power and sexuality.

Foucault argues that power isn't only located in sexual acts, but also in discourses on sexuality. Moreover, discourses on sexuality have been a central way in which power in Western culture has been constituted, particularly with the rise of the bourgeoisie. The new middle classes, as they rose to economic, and – later – political, power, developed a belief-system focused very much on 'the family'. Integral to their beliefs were discourses on hygiene, health, sexuality – a whole new discourse on the body that was pivotal to their own wider role in political relations in the state and economy. Foucault argues that the constitution of our subjectivity is integrally bound up with sexuality. Sexuality in turn is defined by language and discourse in certain ways that are also premised on power relations.

So Sarah Maguire's identity was very much bound up with her sexuality – and this was in turn defined by the conflicting discourses of patriarchal heterosexuality and radical feminist lesbianism. Her ultimate choice of subject position was thus focused on her body through a number of power relations operating through these two discourses. Feminism had enabled her to 'shift the terms of the struggle'. But you might like to consider why one discourse won the day over the other – was it that one was far more powerful, endorsed by social institutions? Or was it her unconscious desires which swung the balance?

There is no final proof of 'truth' of either, of course; both are theoretical perspectives and relate to the wider debate about social constructionism versus essentialism.

▶ ACTIVITY 23 ◀

Think of some other examples of discourses that exist primarily through control/policing of bodies.

COMMENT

One that sprung to my mind was the controversy over child sexual abuse in the Cleveland crisis. Much of the focus of this was on the child's body – whether or not anal dilatation as described in medical discourse was an adequate sign of buggery, regardless of any verbal evidence by children, social workers or parents. Medical discourse is a very important way in which our bodies are subjected to power relations as objects of knowledge and investigation.

Another example would be the ways in which medical discourse pressurizes women to have their babies in hospital, even though they may prefer to have them at home. The 'safety' of the baby is put at risk, it is argued, if women don't have their babies in hospital. But hospitals themselves carry risks – from disease and injury caused by medication or the medical process ('iatrogenic disease'). Induction, generally carried out for the convenience of the hospital staff, can be unpleasant and even dangerous for the mother. Sheila Kitzinger has challenged medical discourse on childbirth through an alternative discourse of 'natural childbirth'. Feminism, too, has challenged patriarchal assumptions inherent in medical discourse on women generally and childbirth in particular.

► **ACTIVITY 24** ◄

An important aspect of Foucault's theory is his claim that 'wherever there is power there is resistance'. One example would be the natural childbirth movement mentioned above. Think of some others.

COMMENT

Perhaps one of the most dramatic examples of women's resistance in recent years was at the Women's Peace Camp at Greenham Common. Unarmed and with no economic back-up, a small handful of women challenged the Western military complex at that base. They resisted existing power relationships by constantly re-defining power and those relationships. An apparent lack of central organization or hierarchy, combined with a diversity of original tactics, thoroughly confused the police and military at the time.

> Now read pp. 279–82 up to '... created in every confrontation', paying particular attention to Foucault's critique of the 'natural' and 'normal'.

For Foucault, as for many feminists, the important point here is that the so-called 'natural' is challenged as being just a social construct. The category of 'woman' was constructed using medical discourse about women's bodies (particularly menstruation and reproduction) as a 'pathological' social category in an attempt thereby to keep close control of the population through families.

> Martin suggests that the 'sexual revolution' of the 1960s was in fact very oppressive for women. Do you agree?

Of course, there's no right answer here at all. The wide availability of the pill meant that pregnancy was not the threat or danger (but also perhaps the protection from unwanted sex?) that it had been for earlier generations. I can certainly remember being told by left-wing men that offering sex to them was a 'duty' or even a 'revolutionary act'. Some women seem to have found it genuinely liberating, others much less so. Here are two quotes from Sara Maitland's book, *Very Heaven: looking back at the 1960s*, which give an idea of two different impressions. The first is by Sara Maitland, the second by Sue O'Sullivan:

> 'Clearly we were entirely wrong in a belief that if we smoked enough dope and screwed enough people the world would be transformed, the revolution brought in, and Eden replanted, but the fact is – whatever she says now – re-reading *The Female Eunuch* it is clear that Germaine Greer did not go around without her knickers for hedonistic delight alone, nor did the Oz editorial people publish pictures of Rupert Bear with his cock out for pornographic motives. Libertarianism was of course fun at least for a great number of women, but part of the fun was the conviction that it was brave, important and socially useful, liberating at a global level, to do these things.'

'I almost made it into the sixties a virgin. But I'd been picked up and enthusiastically fucked by an "older man" while visiting New York City for the first time during the week after graduating from high school. Classically, that first fuck was a huge let down... A huge chasm opened up between my desires and my sexual practice... I'm amazed now when I think of the sexual acrobatics I performed back then with no pleasurable outcome – I could move my hips for hours, take it on all fours, fuck fast and furious, be on top, be stimulated by hand or mouth, grudgingly suck someone off and never a glimmer of the pleasure I felt in anticipation or in fantasy.'

Martin cites Rich's article mentioned earlier which has been extremely important in arguing that women have to be, more or less, forced into heterosexuality. This would seem to conflict with Maguire's account and, to some extent, with Chodorow's.

> Both Rich and Chodorow put a lot of stress on the importance of mothering, yet come to very different conclusions. How do you think this can be explained?

Chodorow, as you may remember from Chapter 4 of *Knowing Women*, is an American sociologist whose work has been influential for its feminist reinterpretation of Freudian theory. She argued that little girls never cut their ties with their primary carer, usually the mother, unlike boys who develop their sense of self in contradistinction to the mother, thus repressing their caring and relational capacities. Girls, according to Chodorow, never wholly do this, and that, she argues, is why women still want to mother. Chodorow thus sees heterosexuality in women and the desire to mother as a result of early socialization, and not as a result of unconscious forces or desires (as psychoanalysts would argue), or as a result of historical and political forces.

On the other hand, Adrienne Rich, a poet and critic, argues that heterosexuality is politically imposed on girls. She believes that little girls, whose first attachment is to the mother, would prefer close relationships with women in later life rather than with men. Heterosexuality she sees not as something natural, but as part of a patriarchal society that has to enforce the institution of motherhood by enforcing heterosexuality on to girls and women. She also differentiates between the patriarchal *institution* of motherhood, and the actual joy and pleasures which women can get from mothering. Mothering is thus very much a political concept for Rich, while for Chodorow, an academic writing within sociological discourse, it is taken-for-granted. A frequent criticism of Chodorow has been that her theory cannot explain homosexuality and lesbianism. Rich, on the other hand, has often been criticized for being an essentialist.

> Now read to the end of Article 6.2, taking note of the most important points about the problems for feminism of the concept 'woman'.

Foucault, Lacan and the post-structuralists argue that there is no essential 'self' – woman or man. This, however, runs against the beliefs of cultural feminists like Adrienne Rich, Dale Spender and Mary Daly. Cultural feminists believe the category of 'woman' is vital politically as well as being an area where women need to empower themselves through close contact with nature, childbirth and, above all, other women and lesbian sexuality.

Martin believes that cultural feminism is dangerous because it separates women from culture and society and falls in to the old humanist trap of claiming that the individual can be separate from society. Politically it means we can't intervene in the processes which create and change meaning because it takes them as already determined and fixed. This could lead to accepting existing definitions of women as passive, close to nature, a victim, irrational.

SUBJECTIVITY AND IDENTITY

▶ ACTIVITY 25 ◀

What do you see as the way out of this conflict? It might be useful to think back to Book Two and jot down some examples of women's oppression in the material world. If we did not have the concept of 'woman', how might these oppressions be understood and explained?

COMMENT

Presumably class, ethnicity and age could go a fair way in explaining some of them partially. But what about phenomena like the 'double shift'? Prostitution? Mothering? Rape? Surely much of this would be rendered invisible without the concept 'woman'? That, essentially, is Martin's main criticism of Foucault and post-structuralism. For Foucault, 'woman' is just another discourse. There is no easy answer, which is why it is an issue that goes right to the heart of feminist debate.

SUMMARY

1. Unconscious desires never exist in a historical vacuum, according to Hollway, but are socially and politically mediated.

2. Power relations, according to Foucault, are woven throughout our lives and relationships. They constantly define and re-define and control our bodies, thoughts and interactions.

3. This process operates through a number of discourses prevalent at any given time. A discourse is an amalgam of facts, beliefs, rules and norms which lays claim to being 'true' within a broad area. But there is never any ultimate 'truth', only a number of discourses which often conflict with and contradict others. This is distinctly different from 'totalizing' theories, such as Marx and Freud put forward, that lay claim to an ultimate 'truth' or universality.

4   Hollway argues that we occupy 'subject positions' within discourses as a result of an interplay between unconscious desires and discourses.

5   Heterosexual relationships, according to Hollway, are subject to discourse and are the site where gendered subjectivity is created and recreated. This takes place through the processes of projection and introjection – splitting.

6   The central discourse of our culture focuses on sexuality and controls and regulates the population through knowledge, introspection and control of pleasure *via* bodies.

7   According to Foucault and the post-structuralists, the notion of 'woman' is only another discourse and 'woman' does not exist. It is seen as an essentializing concept. This conflicts with cultural feminists' view that the concept is vital to women's identity and political struggle.

3
CHAPTER 7
EXPERIENCE AND THE POLITICS OF IDENTITY (WEEK 23)

INTRODUCTION

In the previous chapter you looked at some accounts of how our identities as women and men are shaped by the way in which we align ourselves with particular emotional structures and sets of ideas about gender differences. These distinctions between femininity and masculinity we experience as *personal* characteristics, which of course they are. But the point of Foucault's analysis of how our subjectivities are socially shaped is that our sense of the personal arises from historical processes. It is a social construction and not something innate to our personality. Our identities as women, as mothers, as workers, are constructed through the process of each of us occupying – more or less happily – the social definitions which make up our world. This is far from a straightforward process, for many of the expectations that lie behind the identity of 'woman' are impossible and contradictory. Nonetheless, we juggle the competing expectations that map the contours of wife, mother, lover, worker, student and so on. We make subjective alignments with particular representations of gendered subjectivity which in turn influence our experience of the world and our relationships to other people.

But that of course is only half the story. The meaning of identity is constantly negotiated between competing representations and discourses. Think, for example, of the identity of 'the single parent' which is often publicly debated and contested. Government bodies, pressure groups, social policy analysts and feminist researchers are among some of the groups which attempt to define the nature and status of single parenthood. People who are themselves single parents also contribute to these debates, often as very unequal voices and with limited power to impose their definition. However, it is from the vantage point of that identity that they can participate in the construction of meaning, however unequally. It is also from that identity that people deal with the contradictions between being empowered to act and constrained by the relations of power which impose identity. These relations of power – of economic, political and discursive hierarchies – invariably mean that identities are sustained and reinforced insofar as they contribute to those power relations.

Certainly, in the early 1990s, there is an account of 'the single parent' which prevails over others and which affirms the dominant idea of the non-interventionist state. This account stresses that the single parent is usually a woman who is not financially supported by a man and who therefore makes demands of the state. This view tends to see single parents as a social problem, generated by the breakdown of the family. The 'solution' to the problem, so its advocates argue, is either to reinforce the family, or to enforce more rigidly paternal economic obligations, or both. Clearly, such a definition of the single parent is one which defends the idea that the state should not have to economically support particular kinds of families. Thus behind this idea of a single parent is the hidden assumption that public funds should be allocated to other, more worthy causes.

Some feminist research, however, departs from this dominant view by identifying single parents as women who, in many cases, do not wish to live with the father of their children. In this case single parents are represented as women who, despite the many difficulties it entails, *choose* to be single parents.

Single parents are recognized as legitimate and as having particular needs to which a civilized society should do its best to attend. This mode of identifying single parents is clearly in competition with the more usually accepted account. These polarized constructions by no means exhaust the matter and other representations jostle to characterize single parenthood.

The *experience* of being a single parent is one which is negotiated within these dominant ideologies. Clearly, the prevailing view does not represent adequately the realities which make up single parenthood because it defines those realities in a particular way. Insofar as people experience their lives outside those explanations, these aspects of their social existence can seem idiosyncratic, something only to do with them, and not part of an identity they share with others. Before the emergence of the women's liberation movement, for example, many women individually experienced the reality of sexual oppression and subordination, but as *their* problem. It was a problem which, as Betty Friedan (1963) pointed out, had no name. It was not part of women's identity, and feminism had to engage in a political struggle to redefine that identity so that it included an account of how women actually experienced the world. It was only through constructing this identity that women were able socially and politically to recognize this experience. Without this social construction women's experience remained invisible.

Similarly, many single parents are actually attempting, in different ways, to redefine the relations between women and men. The struggle to represent these changes, to define them, is a struggle to redefine and give different meaning to these identities.

So the relationship between identity and experience is a complicated one. One thing you have been doing in your Personal Workbook is charting this relationship, noting down how you approached the course, identifying who you were then, and how, if at all, doing the course has changed your experience of yourself. You may represent and identify yourself differently and hopefully be aware of how our identities are socially constructed, and collectively and politically experienced. There is no doubt that doing a university degree is a process which imperceptibly alters how you experience the world, as well as altering your identity. To be a university graduate is to enter a very particular construction imbued with worthiness and status. To study women's studies on the other hand, in some quarters at least, may lead to the imposition of a rather different mantle, one generally seen in more ambiguous light, as a less noble enterprise which is somewhat politically dubious. The identity of being a women's studies student is often a hostile one, and one which you no doubt have had cause to consider by this point in the year. Women's studies remains a politically contentious subject – unlike maths or sociology – because it includes the idea of challenging prevailing definitions of women, and of formulating new identities for women. Neither the identity of being a women's studies student nor the subject matter of women's studies are neutral; they are contentious because they make explicit the interest in the politics of definition and the politics of experience.

> At this point you should go back to the Introduction to Book One and read the section on 'The politics of identity' (pp. 8–9).

Our identity as women and men, however, is only one aspect, albeit an important one, of our identities as historical subjects, as people living in a particular time and place according to the conventions and politics of the period. Our identities are not limited to our femininity or masculinity. They are also shaped by our differing experiences of class, sexuality, race, where we live, how old we are and whether or not we are able-bodied. In this chapter we will be looking at some of these other components of identity and how they intersect with gender. As you will see as you read through the three articles, it was the experience of being a *black* woman or *Third World* woman or *middle-class* woman or *white* woman which posed major political and theoretical questions for feminist accounts of gender identity. It was also the diversity of these experiences which raised the issue of how and by whom was the identity of women being defined within feminist theory and politics.

The key question considered by the articles is how does this broader sense of identity alter our conception of 'women' and what implication does the stress on differences between women have for feminist politics? Each of the authors problematizes the issues of experience and identity by asking questions about the specificity of experience on the one hand, and on the other asking questions about the political consequences of identity.

TIMETABLING

There are three articles to study this week as well as the introduction to the chapter. In terms of reading time, each of the articles should be treated equally.

OBJECTIVES

By the end of the chapter you should be able to:

1. Give a detailed account of the problems raised by using the general category 'women', and show what gains are made by the idea of a feminism of difference.
2. Outline the way in which racism is an issue for white women no less than for black women, and an element in the constitution of both white and black identities.
3. Show how the concept of agency has been adopted as a way of analysing subjects as actively engaging with their historical circumstances, and not passively acquiesing to them.
4. Understand critically the relationship between experience and identity.
5. Be able to account for the idea of a 'situated knowledge' and the politics of location.

IDENTITY

Although they are addressing similar theoretical ground they do so from different locations and contexts: Razia Aziz analyses the challenge of Black feminism, particularly as this has shaped debates in the UK; Lata Mani looks at the intersections of First and Third Worlds in the production and reception of knowledge about 'Third World' women; and Minnie Bruce Pratt, as a member of the dominant white class in the United States, considers the impact of racism and imperialism on the formation of her identity. In different ways each of the articles is personally challenging, asking not only that we again reconsider our starting-point, but also that we acknowledge our own identity as one located by relations of hierarchy and power. In addition they suggest that identity cannot be a haven or moral resting-place for it is in the very nature of identity that we must always be aware of its social implications and effects. We must, as Razia Aziz suggests, be prepared to ask the question 'identity for what?'

> Now read the Introduction to Chapter 7 (pp. 287–90) and note down what you take to be the key issues of difference that the articles will be addressing.

The three articles raise the questions of 'race', class, location, agency and positionality as central to understanding the diverse experience and identities of women. Each of the contributors writes from within a tradition within feminism which raised the question of relations of power *between* women and used these concepts in an attempt to analyse these relations. This development marked a major shift in feminist politics and thought which had, up until then, stressed the commonality of women's experience as a group sharing the reality of subordination. In looking at the detail rather than the generality of women's lives, a conceptual shift was inevitable. The concept of location, for example, looks at the relationship between the production and reception of knowledge by and about women. It suggests that 'truth' is not abstract and true for all time, but rather is relative to the way in which knowledge is developed and disseminated by and to women. The concept of agency also militates against generalizations about women by focusing on how certain women dealt with, or reacted to, particular historical circumstances. This is closely related to the idea of positionality which is the idea that women are grounded by very precise configurations of social relationships and events and it is those which exercise influence over those women and not some general status of being a woman.

Earlier understanding of women's position was concerned not with differences between women but with what was understood as 'the' fundamental difference, that between women and men. Much of this earlier discussion had talked about 'women' and 'men' as homogeneous categories between which there were antagonistic or contradictory relations. It was the relationship of power between men and women which had preoccupied feminist thinking, and it was this emphasis which allowed for the construction of women as a non-differentiated theoretical category, as well as political identity. This way of classifying difference often meant that debate became trapped within the either/or parameters of social constructionism vs essentialism. For as long as the social category of gender paralleled the biological category of sex, the question of *gender* identity hovered between the mutually exclusive poles of essentialism and social constructionism.

Looked at through the prism of *identity*, however, the social forces at play in shaping us as social beings make the predominantly social nature of the identities of women much easier to appreciate. If we consider the social, cultural and historical density of identity, it becomes clear that the parallel between sex and gender is not a neat one of equivalence, particularly when gender is seen as one dimension of social identity.

This emphasis on the different identities of women – young/old, black/white, rich/poor and so on – meant that the whole question of the commonality of experience had to be rethought. If women experienced gender in very different ways because of how it was structured by factors of class and race, then it could not be assumed that women would automatically unite as women. Neither could the experience of subordination be 'read off' from gender if the components of identity gave different meaning and different inflections to sexual subordination. This attention to difference seemed to suggest that the idea of commonality had little meaning if women were oppressed in different ways and in some instances, oppressed by other women. As you saw in Chapter 2, Audre Lorde has argued that it is only by recognizing the differences between women that it is possible to see women truly as a group. This is a much more complex notion of political solidarity than the one invoked by appeals to a common experience of gender relations. As you will see as you read through the articles, this closer attention to experience and identity is beginning to give rise to a very different conception of politics itself.

Before you go on to look at the readings, pause for a moment to consider the key concepts in this chapter:

	Key concepts	
identity	class	agency
difference	positionality	politics
'race'		

ARTICLE 7.1 'FEMINISM AND THE CHALLENGE OF RACISM: DEVIANCE OR DIFFERENCE?' BY RAZIA AZIZ

Now read pp. 291–9 of Article 7.1 by Razia Aziz (up to 'Beyond the debate'). Pay particular attention to her use of the term 'race' and note down what you think were the main challenges of Black feminism.

Aziz frames her analysis with a quote from Sojourner Truth and an account of contemporary Black feminism. In both instances black women are saying that the realities of slavery and racism mean that their 'woman-ness' is located by very specific conditions which are profoundly different to those faced by women outside those conditions. Indeed as the extraordinary words of Sojourner Truth make clear, her life was such a denial of the dominant conventions of femininity that it refuted absolutely the essentialist arguments which underwrote those conventions. Slavery was concerned with extracting hard physical labour from women and men alike, and the brutality of the system made little distinction between women and men. Yet even in this context women had to bear the specific exploitation of sexual abuse and seeing their children born into an impossible life. Her gender, class and blackness all defined her reality as a woman, but in a way that had little or nothing to do with the dominant essentialist definitions of womanhood. Not only did Sojourner Truth's experience make a nonsense of these ideas of the nature of women, but the way in which she fought her own predicament completely belied the idea of woman as passive victim. She was not a victim but an adversary of the political system, and her words continue to inspire other women nearly a century and a half later.

Aziz suggests that to understand Sojourner Truth as a historical figure it is important to see her not as a *victim* of a savagely racist society, but as someone who both dealt with and challenged that reality. In other words we must consider individual women (and men) as agents, as people who respond to, and act within, their own historical circumstances and, in so doing, affect those circumstances. We are all of us constituted as subjects of history, moulded by class, gender and race shaping our subjectivity. It is from these parameters that we act on the world, either conserving existing realities or attempting to transform them. (As you will see from the next article, however, the question of women's agency is not always straightforward.)

In citing Truth, Aziz is making the point that Truth's understanding of difference and specificity is one that was lost to feminism and is only now being rediscovered. Within the women's movement black women found it necessary to insist on their own specificity, on their experience of racism and class, and on their sense of difference from white women as an ethnic group. Moreover they stressed that their struggles against racism were often ones which united them with black men and against white women. Both of these claims undermined the idea that there was a natural alliance and identification between women. They also raised the question of power and the politics of identity.

This challenge was a deeply shocking one for many white women for whom the reality of domination was anathema, and for whom the politics of identity has been assumed in the concept of sisterhood. But it was something which white women had to recognize – that racism did not just implicate people with black skin but also those with white skin. The idea of 'race' was constructed from the same ideological storehouse as the idea of sexual natures, and with similar purpose. Both 'theories' imposed a division through hierarchy and both detracted attention from the social and historical conditions which sustained particular, and intersecting, relations of power. Moreover both made the dominant group, be they men or white people, the group from which all social values were generalized. In other words the language of 'race' is the language of domination, and it is only through white women recognizing their place in this system of domination, that feminism can fully dislodge itself from racism. In some respects this was the most difficult of challenges for white women to meet because it required that they rethink their identity in terms of whiteness or – what is the same thing – in terms of power and privilege.

▶ ACTIVITY 26 ◀

Stop for a moment and think about your own whiteness or blackness. Think about how being white is seen as not being coloured. If you are white, how aware of this are you? To what extent do you think of racism as something that black people have to deal with? To what extent do you think black people are thought of as 'victims' of racism?

COMMENT

These were some of the questions that Black feminists asked of white feminists. They rejected the status of 'victim' which emerged as long as white feminists thought of racism as something to do with black people. Black feminists argued that contemporary black women struggle against the racism which dominates their lives – as Sojourner Truth did before them. Their challenge was to question whether white feminists were in fact adversaries of racism. As long as feminism saw the question of race as something external to it, feminism was participating in the construction of black women as victims, as the owners of racism. This was to identify black women as 'other'. And it was only through black women challenging these constructions that feminism became aware of the way it too was participating in the constructions of a racist and sexist society.

The construction of black women as 'other', as inferior or deviant, is one which black women have to confront both within and without the women's movement. And what Aziz is arguing, echoing both Sojourner Truth and Audre Lorde, is that the history of all groups subjected to racist domination is a history of the way in which people fought such restrictions and limitations. In this sense the concept of difference is grounded in the material reality of peoples' lives and predicated on the political conviction that people are agents of their own lives, not victims of history. In other words, identity is not just pre-given but achieved through people claiming their rights to define their own identity and to change their experience.

The parallels between the struggles of black women and a predominantly white feminism are clear. Feminism too rejected the myth of otherness, passivity and victimhood and instead argued that women were persons who, collectively and individually, engaged with and fought against the reality of sexual subordination. Their history was hidden, denied by the mythology of passivity, and their fight to belie the mythology created a new identity for women.

There, however, the parallels ceased as long as feminism failed to recognize that sexism was only one of the vocabularies of subordination. As Aziz points out, there was within feminism the tendency to universalize and assume that as women we shared a collective reality. As black women made clear, however, racism was *also* a collective reality but one which divided women as white and black, superior/inferior, same/other and through all the other hierarchies of domination. In short, the challenge of racism is that feminism must deal with whiteness and domination as well as racism and racialization (the process of objectification of the 'other' which is central to racism). The concept of difference is one which requires that all the material, cultural and political circumstances of women's lives be acknowledged, and this is no less true for 'white' than for 'black' women. Thus, for white women, identity must involve a negotiation of their own place of power in a racist society. Racism, in other words, includes white women, implicating their subjectivity in the myriad of unconscious and conscious presumptions of the dominant group. In this sense it represents a political problem that belongs to white women no less than to black women, and the racialization of whites as superior is something that white feminism has to deal with.

But the terminology of 'black' and 'white', as Aziz says, is also tainted by its origins in racist discourses. In racist or naturalistic discourses they represent homogeneous racial groups. But these groups are neither races nor are they homogeneous. Both are heterogeneous combinations of people who are marked by different historical patterns of power and domination. That this should be recognized was yet another challenge posed by Black feminism, for the emphasis on sisterhood and solidarity had also masked the divisions of class, culture and history between white women. Thus white women had to recognize not only their particular place in racist societies – their whiteness *and* otherness, but also the other divisions that intersected them as a group. It is only by doing this that it becomes possible to see just how multifaceted the struggles against sexual subordination are and, perhaps more importantly, it is only by acknowledging the precise difference of white privilege that it can genuinely be rejected. This is the significance of the concept of difference: understanding, *in its specificity*, the nature of our historical formations as subjects. The problem remains, however, as to how we construct alliances across the histories of difference when those histories themselves shape us through division, power and domination.

> Now read from 'Beyond the debate' to the end of the article (pp. 299–305) and note down what you understand Aziz to be advocating in the concept of identity.

There are two ways in which Razia Azia defines identity. The first is theoretical, the second political. The first definition views identity as something which arises out of the particular material, cultural and political circumstances which construct differences between women and inflect the experience of women. Being black in a racist society in which white people are the dominant group means that black women experience themselves and the world through the dominant ideas of racial inferiority, through ideas of 'otherness' which suggest that black women are fundamentally different, as well as through more overt forms of racism. Black women experience their identities in a world which deals in racist sexual stereotypes, which measures out the worst economic deal to non-whites, sustains institutional racism, and advocates ideas of nationalism which are racist and exclusionary. These components of black identity make up the process of the social construction of identity and it is this construction which must be de-constructed in order to show the relations of power which rest upon it. Such an approach shows exactly how such definitions and practices support the interests of particular groups and particular systems of domination.

The second sense in which Razia Aziz uses the term identity is to indicate the way in which we represent our political identities to ourselves. In actively identifying as <u>B</u>lack women, black women are challenging the racist construction of their identity by insisting on their collective power to fight such ways of being identified. Identity in this sense is about women's political ability to define their own lives, and to produce their own definitions of what it means to be a black woman. But, as Black feminism has so clearly illustrated, we cannot afford to be complacent about our political identities and they too must always be examined for exactly who they are excluding and including. But although the process of de-constructing must be an ongoing one, it must not undermine the possibility of collective representation.

Aziz recognizes that the question of identity is a difficult one and that there is no easy solution to the recognition of difference. She reminds us of the grand narratives of modernity with which feminism grappled for so long. In identifying patriarchy as the systematic way in which women were subordinated, feminism tried to marry patriarchy with class as the other prime mover of history. In the end, however, it was deemed to be an unhappy marriage because the conceptual framework of both narratives could not properly account for the complex reality of women's lives. This complexity could not be reduced to either class or patriarchy or even a combination of class and patriarchy because these accounts of history left out questions of subjectivity and sexuality, of the social construction of the body, of language and meaning, of the unconscious and difference, of 'black' and 'white', of power and pleasure, and identity and difference. In short, feminism needed a broader vocabulary in order to be able to comprehend the reality of women.

Feminism created its own post-modernist discourse through on the one hand critically distancing itself from the dominant (some would say anti-feminist) post-modernist tradition, at the same time as sustaining the dialogue between theory and politics and recognizing the need for collective political action. Thus feminist post-modernism necessarily straddles a contradiction: it advocates a strategy of deconstruction *and* acknowledges the need for women to politically (and personally) represent themselves as black women, lesbian women, working-class women, white women, old women etc., that is to collectively represent themselves. These delineations of identity are exclusive to particular groups of women. But they also outline the specific ways in which subordination and subjugation are experienced and create the common ground on which particular women can struggle against their shared realities. Thus to call oneself lesbian, black or disabled is to claim an identity as well as simultaneously rejecting the dominant constructions of that identity. What Aziz is suggesting is that it is only as long as we are aware of just what has gone into the formation of our subjectivity and how it is interlaced with relations of domination and subordination, that we can begin fully to take hold of our identities as historical agents capable of challenging the dominant relations of power. As she says, we need both to deconstruct our subjectivities and assert our political identity. As you will see in the following articles this is a very demanding and exacting process.

In the next article Lata Mani attempts to think through these issues in a global context.

ARTICLE 7.2 'MULTIPLE MEDIATIONS ...' BY LATA MANI

▶ ### ACTIVITY 27 ◀

Before reading Article 7.2, I want you to stop for a moment and note down your thoughts on the practice of *sati* or widow burning. In particular think about how you see a society in which such things are allowed to occur. You could also note down your view of the women who end their life in such a way, and how you think such actions are to be understood.

COMMENT

Perhaps you thought that practices such as *sati* were found in traditional societies where women were without rights and at the mercy of their husbands. Very often we think of such societies as 'backward' – as measured, that is, against modern societies which guarantee women's rights as individuals. Perhaps too you thought of women who commit *sati* as somehow beyond reason because so bound by custom and convention. Or maybe you thought of such women as weak, as refusing to exercise independent judgement, refusing to choose survival in preference to death. Certainly all these thoughts – sometimes involuntarily – crossed my mind in considering *sati* and one of the points Lata Mani brings out in her piece is the political origin of such views, as well as their continuing political currency. Her article also makes clear that we must be aware of how such constructions, often unacknowledged, can shape our analysis of the position of particular groups of women.

Now read Article 7.2 and think about what Mani means by a politics of location. We will come back to this question again at the end of the discussion.

Mani's opening vignette at the acupuncturist illustrates wonderfully how feminist research is so often received. (No doubt you will have cause to think back upon this quote if or – as women's studies students inevitably are – when you are being genially interrogated about women's studies, your own dubious status as an authentic woman, and your explanation of sexual subordination.) Mani was invalidated as an Indian woman because, according to the acupuncturist, she was Westernized and therefore ever beyond the traditionalism of Indian society. She was inauthentic, a hybrid. So located she could not possibly (according to this theory of knowledge) know about women in India. Her account of her research was received into the acupuncturist's framework which accepted the cultural integrity of practices such as *sati*, on the basis that the culture gave it a significance which made it acceptable. As an outsider neither she nor he could understand this significance. This ostensibly tolerant acceptance of difference was, in Mani's view, based on an underlying assumption of superiority and a perception of traditionalism as a problem of non-Western societies.

Mani gives other examples of the reception of her work which were dependent on the geopolitical context of her audience. This context gave rise to specific interpretations of her research, and to specific identifications of her as an intellectual. Being seen through the Western stereotype of the Indian woman or the Indian stereotype of the Westernized woman made her aware of how both knowledge and identity are inflected by the politics of location. The experience of delivering her research in different cultural and political contexts illustrated the way in which location qualified what it is that is known. Whereas in India the identification with colonialism was minimal, in the West this was a primary consideration. In India her inauthenticity was identified through the definition of being a Westernized intellectual, in America through the construct of the traditional Indian woman. In both cases she was identified as a woman in the language of colonialism and post-colonialism, a process for her which raised the questions of the impact of colonialism on culture and gender formations.

It was this critical perspective which emerged from Mani's experience of being a Third World intellectual working in the First World which gave her a particular appreciation of the death of Roop Kanwar. Mani's feminist perspective arose out of an understanding of her own location and it was this which alerted her to analysing the precise situation faced by Roop Kanwar. The public political language used in discussing the merits and status of *sati* was one which reflected the competing interests of the advocates of traditionalism and those of modernity. Within the debate the identity of Roop Kanwar became a vehicle for political interests. Feminist contributors exposed these interest groups, and the view of women they held, and showed that the power bases of both traditionalism and modernity were grounded in subordinating women. It was not the case that the colonial imposition of liberalism and democracy had produced rights for women. Modernity could not be seen as an obvious improvement on traditionalism if historically it had actually reinforced the practice of *sati*, and, in the case of Roop Kanwar, had only produced a fretful debate on whether she was complicit in, or coerced into, her death. What emerged from this debate was not an extension of rights for women but an extension of state powers to determine whether specific cases of *sati* involved complicity or coercion.

Mani points out how the debate on *sati* demands a reconsideration of the question of agency. To stress, as Razia Aziz did, the need to recognize the agency of women in the most oppressive of circumstances, has dubious merit in a context where such 'agency' is punished by law. Equally, however, to stress the immense social constraints on women's agency is to invite the status of victim. Lata Mani does not pretend to have a solution to this dilemma except to say that we must be aware of the specificities of women's lives and the very contradictory forces which construct this specificity. It is for this reason that feminist knowledge must be situated, and not something which deals in generalities and abstractions. For it is this latter form of knowledge which allows the actual reality of women's lives to be ignored. In the next chapter we will return to this question of the relationship between general and particular knowledge.

ARTICLE 7.3 'IDENTITY: SKIN BLOOD HEART' BY MINNIE BRUCE PRATT

Now read Article 7.3. How would you say Minnie Bruce Pratt's notion of identity echoes that of Lata Mani?

Both authors are in fact quite close in their perspectives. Minnie Bruce Pratt acknowledges that to understand people it is necessary to locate them within the historical contours of their identity, and to recognize at the same time that we are also situated by those historical contours. However much we may wish to be known 'for ourselves', our home and origins are powerful anchors of our identities and they are not ones we can easily discard. Feminists are committed to change but very often this is seen in terms of changing things in the outside world. But the outside world produces our inner sense of self, our identities. It is not possible, she argues, to cast aside those identities because or their political origins, nor is it possible to assume the more politically acceptable identities of others. Rather, as a white woman, she argues that she has to deal with exactly how her formation as a middle-class woman in a racist society has limited and distorted her experience. In exploring her own location, or her home as she calls it, Minnie Bruce Pratt identifies the emotional consequences of being a member of a dominant group, in the half-buried fear of those not like her or her folk. Such fear arises not from difference but from domination, the fear that it will be seen for what it is, rather than through the rationalizations of power.

Having been forced to recognize herself as part of a dominant group Pratt traces the various cogs of her identity – liberal student, married student, wife, mother, woman. In reflecting on her life from the vantage point of her identity as feminist, she was able to reconstruct another history of her home and origins, one which recognized that her sense of security and belonging derived from the insecurity and marginalization of others. But dislodging the powerful constraints of fear and hostility that being part of a dominant group imposed was not easy. Pratt suggests that it is not a question of re-locating oneself in another identity but of reappropriating one's own history through challenging those aspects of it which distort and undermine. Here we have yet another conception of agency based not on some abstract notion but on a consideration of the specificity of a life and the history of an identity formation.

SUMMARY

In each of the articles in this chapter the questions of experience, identity, agency and positionality have been grounded in the material, political and cultural reality of women's lives. This way of locating difference is one which refuses to make generalizations about women and instead focuses on the circumstances which determine women's lives and which in turn allow a greater or lesser degree of space for women to confront and negotiate their circumstances. This emphasis on specifying exactly what is meant by 'women' is also a way of highlighting the diverse social forces that construct identity and shape experience. It is also proposed by the three authors as a way of identifying the strategies women should adopt to challenge their subordination. From this standpoint, situated knowledge and the politics of location are the precondition to solidarity amongst women because it is only through acknowledging difference that real alliances between women can be developed.

■ ■ ■

Now turn to Study Guide 4 to prepare for your work on Book Four, *Imagining Women*.

4
CHAPTER 8
THE AIMS AND ACHIEVEMENTS OF FEMINIST THEORY
(WEEK 31)

TIMETABLING

This week is a full one for you. It is the week in which you will complete your study of *Knowing Women* and begin studying the Course Conclusion. This Study Guide will take you through Chapter 8 of *Knowing Women* and help you with re-reading the book's Introduction. I would suggest that you put aside the equivalent of one longish evening's work for the Introduction to Chapter 8 and its first article by Sandra Harding (this also involves reviewing an article by her that you read in *Inventing Women*). You may then need a slightly shorter time for the book Introduction and the final article by Elizabeth Gross.

INTRODUCTION

This final chapter of *Knowing Women* is concerned with the claims feminist theory can make for itself. In what sense can it claim to produce knowledge which is superior to that produced by the theories it criticizes as biased and male-centred? Can feminist theory claim to be unbiased, to produce an objectively true view of the world? Or should it accept that no view is unbiased and that no knowledge is any more true than any other? Or are there specific reasons which might make feminist theories superior? Is the knowledge they produce in some sense more true or less biased?

The claims that feminist theory can make for itself are, of course, related to the type of critiques such theories make of the knowledge claims of other theories. In Book Three, in considering feminist critiques of scientific theories, you examined the claims that existing science was making for itself. The issue was then raised of what a science improved by attention to feminist criticisms would be like. Would it follow current scientific method better than existing science by removing its biases? Or would meeting the feminist criticisms involve completely reformulating the methods of scientific practice and the claims made for it? Similar issues arise for all theorizing, in the social sciences as well as the natural sciences, and it is in this broader context that we shall consider them here.

One of the readings for this week is an article by Sandra Harding on the aims of feminist theory. You read another article by her in Chapter 1 of *Inventing Women* called 'How the women's movement benefits science: two views', which forms a good introduction to the issues raised this week.

ACTIVITY 25

Skim-read Article 1.4 from *Inventing Women* again and write some notes now on the two perspectives it outlines and what each of them has to say on the contribution women can make to science in general.

COMMENT

Harding talks about two types of feminist critique of science:

1   Those which think that (most) existing science is 'bad science' but can be made good, an approach which Harding calls 'feminist empiricism'. This view shares with mainstream science its methodology and its goal of objectivity but claims that much existing science fails in this respect. According to this view, women have no different contribution to make to science from that of men, because the position of the scientist in society should be irrelevant to the science produced. However, rather inconsistently as Harding points out, proponents of this view also sometimes claim that women may be less prone to bias than men and further that the impact of feminism may help everyone be more sensitive to such biases.

2   Another type of feminist criticism which thinks that all science, that is 'science as usual', necessarily fails in feminist terms, because of its methodology. This latter view rejects the idea that any science can be objective and sees claims to objectivity as just a cover for male bias. All science is in practice grounded in the society in which it arises and incorporates the values and biases of its inventors. According to this 'feminist standpoint' approach, science done from a woman's point of view will be better than existing male-centred science not because it is objective or value-free, but because women's experience is wider and women have less to gain than men from covering up the truth.

Sandra Harding's article in Chapter 8 takes these issues a bit further. In it she not only questions whether science should be seeking to be objective, but also looks at whether there is any reason to claim that a feminist standpoint is superior to any other. The Introduction to Chapter 8 takes up this question in more general terms, making it clear that it is not just an issue about the natural sciences, but about feminist theory in general. It leads us on from the debate between feminist empiricism and feminist standpoint theorists to the question of what sort of theory should replace existing male-centred theory and what sort of claims feminist theory should make for itself.

> Read now the Introduction to Chapter 8, making notes on the following questions as you read:
> What two alternative aims are outlined for feminist theory?
> How would each view criticize the other?

The project of building a feminist successor science is the one that follows on most directly from the feminist standpoint methodology discussed earlier. It states that a feminist science could be built which overcomes many of the problems of existing science and which, by using the insights of women, would be able to claim superiority over other theories not just for women, but in some more universal sense. Post-modern feminism, on the other hand, rejects any theory's claim to universality and, while it endorses feminist critiques of male-centred theories, does not consider that this gives feminist theory the right to claim any privileged access to the truth itself.

Instead, post-modernism disputes the claim of any theory to universal knowledge of 'reality'; all *any* theory can do is look at the world from a particular situated point of view. To attempt to claim more for your own theoretical structures is to use the power inherent in discourse to control the thoughts of others and make them see 'reality' in your way. Against this, feminist standpoint theorists argue that, having developed a critique of male-centred theory, it makes no sense not to claim that feminist theories are superior.

Sandra Harding in her article for this chapter argues that it is neither necessary nor desirable to take a post-modernist or a feminist standpoint position to the exclusion of the other.

ARTICLE 8.1 'THE INSTABILITY OF THE ANALYTICAL CATEGORIES OF FEMINIST THEORY' BY SANDRA HARDING

Read now the first section of Article 8.1, up to the end of page 342. In it, Sandra Harding outlines how feminist theory started by criticizing and transforming a variety of pre-existing theories, none of which had taken women as their starting-point. As you read this section, try to answer the following questions:

How did feminist theory come to realize that claims made by non-feminist theories to represent universal 'man' were illegitimate?

What implications did this have for whether feminist theory could claim to represent any universal woman?

What does Harding think should be the aim of feminist theorizing?

Harding sees a turning-point in the development of feminist theory when it moved on from adapting male-centred theories to building theories which started from the experiences of women. The claims to universality of male-centred theory were then exposed by the recognition that it had always ignored vast areas of the experience of both women and men, such as reproduction and the emotional side of life.

However, having rejected male experience as the basis for knowledge and any corresponding notion of universal man, it then made no sense to claim a universal female experience to stand in its place. Just as the notion of universal man had, by being constructed as having nothing to do with the traditional concerns of women, been shown to be in practice gendered and, further, to misrepresent even male experience, so any supposedly universal notion of woman would in practice be of a particular class, race and culture and would misrepresent women's experience if it failed to recognize this fact.

Harding therefore agrees with post-modernism's suspicion of attempts to claim universality for feminist theories, for inevitably problems will be found with existing theories and there will be women for whom they do not speak and whose experiences are thereby ignored. But she does not agree that this should prevent us from constructing theories piecemeal in as innovative way as possible, recognizing that anything we create will be unstable, just expressing 'what we think at the moment we want to say'.

This is a theme that runs through the rest of her article: the idea that methodological inconsistencies and instability are to be welcomed, rather than solutions found to them once and for all. In the next section she returns to the question of whether feminism should criticize sexist assumptions in scientific research as 'bad science' or recognize that they are simply part of 'science as usual'? In this section, she reiterates the points she made in her other article about the inconsistencies of the feminist empiricist position.

> Read now the next section of Article 8.1 entitled '"Bad science" or "science as usual"?', making notes on the following questions:
>
> How does feminist empiricism claim that sexist bias enters scientific research?
>
> How do claims for the superiority of research done by women, or by feminists, subvert the basis of empiricism?
>
> What does this mean about the approach feminists should take to the concepts and methods of scientific enquiry?

Feminist empiricism claims that sexist bias can enter research in three ways:

(a) in what is seen as needing explanation;
(b) by sexist assumptions affecting what is observed;

(c) through the way the male-dominated scientific community is used to validate research.

But recognizing this causes a problem for empiricism. For, according to empiricism, the social identities of both the researcher and the scientific community are irrelevant to its scientific method and so science should not be sexist. Feminist empiricism not only criticizes male-dominated science for failing to conform to its own rules of scientific method, it also has an explanation of why such failings might be expected to occur. But this explanation undercuts the claim that the sexism of science lies not in its method, but in the failings of its practitioners to carry out that method.

Harding clearly thinks that the only conclusion to draw from this is that the fundamental categories of scientific thought are male-biased, but this does not lead her to conclude that women should give up science altogether. True to her refusal to be forced into taking fixed positions when these are inappropriate, she sees neither a project of redeeming science nor dismissing it altogether as in the best interests of women.

> In the next section, Harding moves on to the debate between post-modernism and those who believe in the successor science project. Read now the section entitled 'Successor science or post-modernism', making notes on the following questions as you read:
>
> How does the feminist standpoint epistemology justify its view that women are the ideal agents of knowledge?
>
> Why does post-modernism question this view?
>
> What criticisms can in turn be made of the post-modernist position?
>
> Which view does Harding support?

Feminist standpoint epistemology sees women as having a more complete vision than men because the work that they do, which includes the reproductive emotional labour that is ignored in male-centred thought, gives women a more complete picture. Men have only a partial view of reality because, as a dominant group, much of their theory is concerned to justify their own domination and hide the 'politically imposed nature of the social relations which they see as natural'. This argument is developed by analogy with that of Marx who saw the working class as having better access to the truth through their labour than the capitalist class, who had to hide the truth in order to justify their own domination. For feminist standpoint theorists, however, it is not the working class through wage labour, but women, through their multifaceted productive and reproductive activities, who are the ideal agents of knowledge.

Post-modernist feminism, on the other hand, thinks that all attempts to impose a conceptual framework on the world, that is to create any epistemology, should be seen as attempts to create methods of policing thought. It therefore does not see the development of a feminist epistemology as an appropriate goal for feminism. Against this, Harding argues that the relativism to which post-modernism leads can be seen as abdicating all responsibility, saying in effect that dominating groups have an equal right to hold their distorted views, and act upon them to oppress others, as those they oppress have to see things differently.

As usual, Harding insists that we do not have to choose one approach or the other. Further, she sees the post-modern approach as potentially appropriate to a world in which thought does not need policing, but not as a way of getting there. She sees the feminist standpoint approach, by legitimating the subjugated knowledge of women as much more effective at challenging the power of existing systems of thought. But above all, she insists we do not have to choose one or the other and should not dismiss the problems each raises about the other approach.

In the next section Harding raises a problem with feminist standpoint epistemology concerning what it has to say about the theories of other oppressed groups.

> Read now the next section entitled 'The feminist standpoint and other "others"', writing notes on the following questions:
>
> What problems arise for a feminist standpoint epistemology once the existence of other axes of oppression is recognized?
>
> Does Harding see a resolution of these problems?

If women have a privileged insight because of the distinctive nature of their experience, what about other oppressed groups? Could not other groups make similar claims about their distinctive experience? Should not there also be a black standpoint epistemology, based on black experience and so on? And if so, what relation should there be between feminist standpoint epistemology and the others?

Harding suggests two possible solutions of this dilemma. The first is to say that feminist standpoint epistemology should stand with other epistemologies, each claiming their own validity as ways of looking at the world, but not at the expense of the others. This would overcome some of the post-modernist criticisms of attempts to police thought, yet retain the idea that the oppressed have superior knowledge to that of the oppressors.

Harding's other solution is for all standpoint epistemologies to give up their claims to be able to produce universal knowledge of the world or express universal goals, because each social group is cross-cut by other divisions. This solution is more in line with the post-modernist scepticism about all claims to universal knowledge.

The final section of Harding's article is a bit different. In it she explores a question which you looked at right at the very beginning of this course: the relation between sex and gender. She uses that dichotomy to explore another theme that has run through this book (and other parts of the course): the way dualistic thinking tends to dominate the way we see the world. Her response is in line with her thinking throughout her paper: that the dilemmas posed are real and that we should regard the instability of thought that arises from them as more of a valuable conceptual resource than a problem.

> Read now to the end of Article 8.1, noting how her views on sex and gender and dualisms in general function as an example of the sort of line of argument she has been pursuing throughout the article.

In this article, as in her previous one, Harding has taken an existing dichotomy (or dualism) and dissolved it. In the earlier article she insisted that despite their apparent contradictions we had to support the projects of both feminist empiricism and feminist standpoint theorists. This time the dualism is between feminist standpoint epistemology and post-modernism, and here Harding claims that the tension between the two views is irresolvable but productive. In this way, Harding is also applying another principle of feminist theorizing, that of challenging established dualisms, insisting that the world does not have to be divided into either/ors.

The Introduction to *Knowing Women* also refers to the debate between post-modernism and feminist standpoint epistemologies. It raises the same issues about feminist theorizing in general, but raises them in a more political vein, focusing on the question of what difference it makes who does the theorizing.

> Although you may have read it before, read now the Introduction to *Knowing Women*, up to the paragraph ending '... all feminist research.'

in the middle of page 5, making notes on the following points as you read.

Rational individualism is used as an example of a picture of universal man which is inherently masculine. What argument based on reproduction is given to support this contention?

What would a totalizing feminist theory want to put in its place?

How does post-modernism criticize this aim and what alternative aims does it have for the feminist project?

Why do feminist standpoint theorists feel that not all essentialisms should be rejected?

How has this debate made women into the knowing subjects of feminist theory?

Rational individualism presupposes that the individuals of which society consists are self-contained and self-seeking agents; that is, they neither depend on, nor do they care for, other individuals. This means that the care of dependent children by parents, or other adults, cannot be explained within this model. However, society cannot continue if some people do not care for the next generation. Real societies are thus structurally dependent on forms of behaviour which cannot be explained by rational individualism. So the behaviour to which the rational individual is supposed to conform cannot apply to all individuals. In practice it is more like that expected of men than women in our society. If people are differentiated by gender and the model is to apply at all, it can only be to the gender that does not care for the children; in that sense the model can be called masculine.

To replace theories based on individualism, a totalizing feminist theory would analyse the structures by which women are subordinated. Such a theory would not respect existing political and theoretical boundaries between public and private. It would show how the two domains are mutually interdependent and that the boundary between them has been historically constructed and is subject to change (or perhaps even abolition).

Post-modernism criticizes the aim of creating totalizing theory, claiming that such theory must inevitably fall into the trap of essentialism. For whenever a grand historical narrative is constructed, it has to call upon some fundamental essence or essences as the underlying force of historical change which explains the diverse changes that are actually observed. Some theories use class struggle, others technological progress, as the underlying force for change; these have been criticized by feminists as incapable of explaining changes within gender relations. Post-modernism claims that a theory based on gender would be no better, for it would just substitute one essentialism for another. Against this, feminist standpoint theorists argue that it is not always the case that essentialisms should be avoided, for the concept of 'woman' itself is an essentialist category. For post-modernists, this means that the category has to be questioned and, in particular, the idea of women having any universally shared defining characteristics cannot be assumed. For feminist standpoint theorists, however, this is to undercut the very basis on which feminism stands, the idea that women as a subordinate gender do have something in common.

Both post-modern feminist and feminist standpoint theorists agree that it matters who does the theorizing. For post-modernism this is because there is no correct vantage point from which the objective truth can be seen and all thought is from a particular subject position; women from their diverse subject positions therefore create feminist theory in all its diverse forms. Feminist standpoint theorists agree that the subject position from which theory is created is important; however, they do not agree that all subject positions lead to equally valid theory. As we have seen, they believe that women, because of their wider experience and subordinate position in society, will create theory that attempts to uncover truths that men have a vested interest in not being able to see.

ARTICLE 8.2 'WHAT IS FEMINIST THEORY?' BY ELIZABETH GROSS

The final article in *Knowing Women* is by Elizabeth Gross and in some ways it functions as a postscript to the book, though from a definite standpoint. Like the Introduction to the book, she starts her article by outlining her view of two phases through which feminist theory has passed.

> Now read Article 8.2 up to the end of the quotation from Finn and Miles on page 359. While you do so, think about the following questions:
> How does Gross characterize the project of the earlier phase of feminist theorizing?
> Why did this project change?
> How does she characterize the current phase?

Gross talks about the earlier stage as one in which feminist theory tried to give women and 'women's issues' equal status with men within patriarchal theory. However, this proved impossible because those theories did not exclude women accidently but were actually based on that exclusion. They could not therefore be expanded to include women, as anything more than substitute men, without fundamental transformation of the theory itself. To be recognized in such theories, equality had to mean sameness, and because this could not be achieved, women could not be included in any meaningful way.

By contrast, Gross characterizes the current phase as one in which feminist theory has sought autonomy for women from the theoretical structures of men. This means claiming the right to accept or reject the theoretical tools of men on the sole grounds of their appropriateness to the way women want to look at themselves. Further, it also means claiming the right to create one's own theory independent of its relation to men's. It means recognizing that women are the subjects of feminist theory, which has its own methods and presumptions and something to say about all objects of study, not just women and women's issues.

In the remainder of her article, Gross outlines what she sees as the new project of feminist theory, as it moves beyond just unearthing and reacting to the sexism of patriarchal theories. As Gross notes, these are fairly speculative ideas, and you many find some of them a bit hard to follow. If you are pressed for time, don't work too hard on the details but try to get the general feel of what she is saying. Gross does take a pretty definite stand on what such an autonomous feminist theory would *not* be. As you read the remainder of her article, think about how you would situate Gross in relation to the debates that you have looked at this week.

> Read now to the end of Article 8.2, thinking about what she says in the light of the debates between post-modernism and feminist standpoint theories? How do Gross's views compare with those of Sandra Harding?

Gross is definitely a post-modernist. Look, for example, at the list of the theoretical commitments of patriarchal adherences questioned on pages 363 and 364. Unlike Harding, then, Gross sees a benefit in taking sides in the feminist standpoint versus post-modernism debate. Gross values the work that has been done to criticize patriarchal theory from within, but sees no mileage in feminists replacing patriarchal theory with a new feminist theory which makes similar knowledge claims for itself. For her, feminism has moved on to a better and more productive phase by embracing autonomy.

The question of whether equality is what feminists should be fighting for was one with which this book started, though in a more practical form. Now we are considering this issue with respect to theory itself. It may well take some time for you to form your own opinions about this. I am certainly not sure exactly what I think about it. After all, as Harding says in her article, you do not have to decide for ever, categories can be unstable; they may just be the best way of expressing 'what we think at the moment we want to say'.

■ ■ ■

This is the end of your work on *Knowing Women* and it is almost, but not quite, the end of your work on this course. Before you finish, however, there is still the Course Conclusion, to which you should now turn and which is designed to help you draw together the main themes of this course.

REFERENCES

CIXOUS, H. (1984) *Writing the Feminine*, Lincoln, NE, University of Nebraska Press.

FRIEDAN, B. (1963) *The Feminine Mystique*, London, Victor Gollancz.

IRIGARAY, L. (1985) *This Sex Which Is Not One*, Ithaca, NY, Cornell University Press.

MAITLAND, S. (ed.) (1988) *Very Heaven: looking back at the 1960s*, London, Virago Press.

MITCHELL, J. (1974) *Psychoanalysis and Feminism*, Harmondsworth, Penguin Books.

RICH, A. (1981) 'Compulsory heterosexuality and the lesbian continuum', *Signs*, Vol. 6, Summer.

RIVIERE, J. (1929) 'Womanliness as masquerade', *International Journal of Psychoanalysis*, Vol 10.

WHITFORD, M. (1989) 'Rereading Irigaray', in Brennan, T. (ed.) *Between Feminism and Psychoanalysis*, London, Routledge.

ACKNOWLEDGEMENTS

p. 15: cartoon from Ros Asquith, *Toddler*, 1989, Pandora Press, by permission of Harper Collins; *p. 16*: Roberts, M. (1986), *The Mirror of the Mother*, Methuen and Co.; *p. 28*: Kantaris, Sylvia (1983) *From the Tenth Muse*, Peterloo Poets, 1983, Menhir Press (re-issue) 1986, © Sylvia Kantaris; *p. 35*: cartoon by Meg Gilbert, first published in *Australian Feminist Studies*, No. 10, Summer 1989, reproduced by permission of the artist.